Recovering My Kid

RECOVERING MY KID

Parenting Young Adults in Treatment and Beyond

Joseph Lee, M.D.
Medical Director, Hazelden Youth Services

HAZELDEN®

Hazelden
Center City, Minnesota 55012
hazelden.org

Library of Congress Cataloging-in-Publication Data

Lee, Joseph, 1975-
Recovering my kid : parenting young adults in treatment and beyond / Joseph Lee.
p. cm.
ISBN 978-1-61649-264-9 (softcover)—ISBN 978-1-61649-453-7 (e-book)
1. Young adults—Substance use. 2. Young adults—Substance use—Prevention. 3. Parenting. 4. Substance abuse—Treatment. 5. Adolescent psychology. I. Title.
HV4999.Y68L44 2012
362.29'13—dc23

2012032365

Editor's note
The names, details, and circumstances may have been changed to protect the privacy of those mentioned in this publication.

This publication is not intended as a substitute for the advice of health care professionals.

Alcoholics Anonymous, AA, and the Big Book are registered trademarks of Alcoholics Anonymous World Services, Inc.

16 15 14 13 12   1 2 3 4 5 6

Cover design: David Spohn
Interior design: Madeline Berglund and Mayfly Design
Typesetting: Mayfly Design
Developmental editor: Peter Schletty
Production editor: April Ebb

Contents

Preface

Out of Love for Our Children

Nothing makes parents' hearts sink faster than the thought of their child suffering. And addiction is a uniquely dark and deep form of suffering. Over years of addiction, families are worn down, trust is lost, and relationships are strained. No logic or science can adequately explain how the disease mutates the afflicted, how they no longer resemble the loved ones who once seemed so familiar. All too often, this is the tragic lens through which society views the young who lose their way.

But that is a book and a story for another time. This book is about something much more hopeful.

In medicine, I have been a humble witness to humanity's enormous capacity for compassion and sacrifice. Whether on an oncology unit or on a psychiatric floor, I have rarely experienced a virtue more profoundly awe-inspiring than the love that parents have for their children. (A child's love for a parent, on the other hand, can be surprisingly conditional.) The lengths to which families will go to help their children give me faith, at least momentarily, in a greater potential for all of us.

Of course, it is delusional not to take note of the strife that accompanies young people in treatment for addiction. Often they are irritable, physically worn, resistant, and lashing out at the world. It can be hard to maintain a sense of emotional objectivity when working with this group.

With all of that in mind, however, we need to make a point to see more than the disease in these youth. When we relate to young addicts at Hazelden, we also remember the wonderment and promise they possessed as small children. We envision them on their first day of school. We remember the thrill of their most memorable achievements and the nostalgic times spent in the company of loved ones. In them lie the collective hopes and dreams of generations past that spark so haltingly now—and the yearning of families to see those dreams rekindled once more.

Our children are our greatest treasures. There is nothing of greater value, nobody for whom we'd sacrifice more. We recognize and celebrate their changes and their maturity from adolescence into young adulthood. And yet our children always remain our children—not because we are naïve, but because we see them through this beautiful capacity for unconditional love. It is in this spirit that I want to connect with you, the reader, in helping those most precious to us.

Acknowledgments

The philosophies set forth in this book have been shaped by those who trained me.

I would like to thank the excellent faculty at Duke University and Johns Hopkins University hospitals for putting up with me as a resident.

In particular, special thanks are due to John Walkup, M.D., whose teachings about parenting have long been a cornerstone of my therapeutic approach. Many of the parenting terms used in this book, including *power struggles* and *expectations*, are borrowed from his instruction.

Special thanks to Doug Toft for his invaluable help crafting this book.

Introduction

The Culture of Families

In some ways, parenting is harder now than ever before. I know people in every generation might say this, but today it really *is* true. I'm not stating this to make anyone feel sorry for our current generation of parents or to pine for the "good old days," as I recognize they may be more nostalgia than reality. Still, this is a topic worth discussing.

When I was growing up, most families had one parent who worked. This isn't a prelude to a speech or a political rant about "family values." The facts are simply that many middle-class American families in the past could get by on one paycheck. And, as a result, parents had more time to spend with their children.

Over the years, I found that my thinking about families changed. I didn't even realize it at first. When I started working with children in residency, I just automatically assumed that both of the parents worked. I didn't see this as a bad thing in and of itself until I started thinking of the ramifications of that change. With most families having two providers, maybe there's less time spent among family members, and maybe our quality of living has changed. I don't have hard facts on this, but as a result of these observations, I'm saddened that limited family interaction has become the norm in our society.

Then there's the issue of maintaining our family culture, free of outside influences. I didn't have a cell phone until I was in medical school. I can't remember how I ever got by without one, but I did. I'm not anti-technology in the least, but in generations past, it was much easier to get "off the grid."

With greater time to spend with their children and more control over what messages got to them, parents in previous generations had an easier time establishing their family cultures, norms, and values. Conversely, with diminishing "face time" with family and 24/7 exposure to the Internet, text messaging, social media, and whatever else, it is harder for parents to get everyone on the same page. This isn't to discourage freedom of thought or creativity, and I'm not suggesting parents should dominate their children's thinking. The truth is, however, that anyone with a bizarre idea can find support for it online, and kids who are addicted to substances will find plenty of ramblings to justify their lifestyle. More than ever before, our children are influenced by others earlier and with increasing frequency. There is greater competition for everyone's time than in the past.

Diminished face time, pinched resources, and an inability to moderate outside influences are growing challenges for modern parents. There is no point in lamenting the facts, though. What we need to do is update our parenting approaches so that we can stay ahead of ever-changing times.

I am really interested in the philosophy behind things. The cornerstone of my clinical work is a firm set of frameworks for understanding what I see on a daily basis. This doesn't mean that I know all the answers, or even half of them. It *does* mean that I can put complicated clinical issues in contexts that are consistent and meaningful.

Too often, parents feel ungrounded because there's simply so much information out there. It's hard to know what's right for our children, or what's even true. Sometimes parents feel like lemmings, led from one hysterical parenting tactic to another:

Feed your kids this, talk to them like that, give them these lessons after school, and play them this kind of music. They are mercilessly subjected to reams of facts and concepts about raising children and expected to remember it all. Worse yet, social and media pressures make parents feel guilty, directly or indirectly, if they don't keep up with the latest trend—never mind whether it's actually helpful. Lacking key contexts for all that information, we can get caught up in minutiae.

Frameworks are designed to prevent this problem. By *framework*, I mean a set of ideas that guide our thinking and behavior. These are broad organizing principles that allow us to file new insights in appropriate mental folders, and then use those insights to make wise choices in daily life. Frameworks allow people to process new information quickly, because there are common reference points, precedents, and contexts.

I present several frameworks in this book, and they all relate to one big idea: *family culture*.

In any decade, there are a few memorable companies that shine above others. People marvel at their success. Books are written about their inner workings, the very mechanisms of their meteoric rise. Of course, the same kind of phenomenon happens in other areas of life. For example, what is it that makes certain sports teams consistently better than others? Why are some school systems better than others, regardless of funding and type of students? The answer comes down to culture.

The whole notion of culture is fascinating, multilayered, and complex. Basically, it refers to the attitudes and behaviors shared by members of any group, small or large. Sports teams have their own distinct cultures. So do schools, companies, communities, and families.

What I recognized during my training at hospitals affiliated with Duke University and Johns Hopkins University is that both institutions foster a successful kind of culture. For example, along an underground transit tunnel connecting two of the buildings on the Johns Hopkins Hospital campus is a row of billboards. Each of the billboards has the cover of the annual *U.S. News & World Report: Best Hospitals* issue. And Hopkins has proudly retained the number one ranking overall for some time now. Sure, this might be criticized as a self-aggrandizing gesture. But no one can deny the impact it has on the people who work there. In fact, I actually noticed that some employees would walk sleepily into the tunnel, peer at the posters, then straighten up and walk briskly, their heads a little higher, their cadence marked with increased purpose. The effect was subtle, and perhaps only noticed by psychiatrists like myself, yet it was there.

The difference between Johns Hopkins and any other hospital is harder to quantify than you might think. It's easy to look at the world-renowned researchers and physicians, the place of Johns Hopkins in the history of American medicine, the research dollars it wins, and the reputation it nurtures—the big-picture differences. But my experience was that many of the physicians at Johns Hopkins were like physicians anywhere else—perhaps a bit brighter but not exceedingly so. This isn't to knock them; it's just to say that with great organizations, the whole truly is greater than the sum of its parts.

I've seen the same kind of trends working with kids in schools in four different states. Some schools are simply better—consistently so, as a matter of fact. Again, the mechanism can be hard to grasp. Although a number of variables contribute to the success of a school, some are independent of funding and the number of computers they have.

Conversely, I have worked with schools where no amount of money could fix a fundamental but difficult-to-pinpoint flaw in their operation.

What I've realized over time is that great organizations have the right kind of culture. It may spring from their attention to detail, their commitment to be the best, a shared mission statement that actually guides people's behavior, or other powerful factors.

The same thing is true of families.

I was listening to the radio the other day and heard a segment about digital textbooks for school. The attraction of such textbooks and the promise they hold from so many perspectives (environmental, for one) drew my attention. But the presenters said something that made me think. Despite the slick presentation and the intuitive notion that technologically savvy tools would be a boon for students, the research thus far actually suggests that use of the latest technology yields little in the way of academic improvement. The presenters found this baffling. I, too, was surprised at first, and then I did some thinking.

I was raised in Seoul, South Korea, until I turned seven. I attended first grade and part of second grade there. Even now, I can remember the competitiveness of my school environment and the many differences in the academic culture—for better and worse—between schools in Korea and the United States. In my Korean school, there were sixty first-graders to a teacher. That kind of ratio would infuriate many parents—and in our country, rightfully so. But somehow, the Korean schools managed. They didn't just manage, in fact; they were ahead in their curriculum when compared to similar schools in the United States. The Korean students were attentive, even in large classes, and many of them thrived. How did this happen?

Well, it didn't have anything to do with computers. My school in Korea didn't have anything high-tech. But there was a distinct culture based on parent involvement in schools and high expectations of children. There were differences in how teachers were respected socially. When I was young, for example, being a teacher in South Korea was akin to being a doctor here in the United States. Not all of the differences were necessarily for the better; Korean teachers also made us do group calisthenics in the morning before classes, which may or may not have had anything to do with results. But aside from having to learn a new language, I was academically well prepared for the transition from South Korea to my elementary school in Norman, Oklahoma.

Perhaps the fact that technology doesn't really improve academic achievement shouldn't surprise us. Perhaps what's lost in conversations about teacher-student ratios, computers, and innovative ways of engaging children is a discussion about the *culture* of a country's educational system. I am willing to wager that, even now, there must be countries that do well by their students without the need of the best technology or the cleverest ways to make learning fun.

Culture, then, is an operational term. It does not pertain to any specific country or ethnicity. Instead, culture is the palpable—but not always readily apparent—sum of shared values that drive behaviors. Different cultures lead some groups of people to different ends than others, regardless of material resources.

As your own child engages in treatment for addiction, you will have the opportunity to examine your own family culture. More than likely, that culture has been passed down to you from your extended families. Your family culture may also have been formed as a reaction to your own experiences while growing up. If you grew up in a volatile environment due to alcoholism or abuse, for example, you might have sworn to create the opposite environment when you had children.

Cultures in families are especially visible during a crisis. *In times of need, people turn to their tried-and-true "playbooks"*—their familiar behaviors and default norms. These norms are passed down from generation to generation. They are fundamental beliefs that shape everything from expectations about expressing emotions to beliefs about valuing money. Marriages can also implode based on diverging ideas and differing family cultures. Some people want to talk openly about problems because that is what their families do; their spouses may want to put their heads down and just work harder at finding peace.

When it comes to parenting, family culture is the bottom line. Family culture influences when and how often children will approach you when they need to talk. Family culture determines whether children choose to share their feelings with you or simply give you a "play-by-play" description of key events. Family culture determines whom your child approaches first—you or your spouse or partner. It shapes how you respond in turn. It also shapes how ashamed your child feels about drug use and mental health issues.

In short, *culture is the key ingredient for preventing your child's drug use and for navigating treatment.*

In radio shows and newspaper interviews, I'm often asked to give tips for parents. The questions are predictable: *What should we say when our kids are showing signs of drug use? How do we go about discussing drugs with our kids?* Sometimes, parents just want suggestions for beginning a conversation with their children. At other times, they seek the magic words that will change their children's minds in an instant and win unequivocal trust.

Unfortunately, life just doesn't work that way.

I emphasize that *parents need to invest in their family culture and maintain it over time*, much as they would invest over the long term in a savings account or a college fund. Only then will the resources be available in a family's time of need. Instead of focusing on what to say at a specific moment, parents need to carefully and consistently—over time—set up the right kind of culture in the home. When that culture is developed, children will know where to turn for help, and parents will know how to respond. Now, as we all know, this isn't a foolproof strategy. But it is the best and most reliable tool that parents have at their disposal.

These days, so many parenting tips are based on superficial matters. The conversations are about finding the right activities, having enough activities, staying cool as parents, learning to talk on your child's level, and the like. I'm not saying these elements are trivial. However, I am saying that the critical factor is taking a fundamental look at the very culture of our homes.

So how do we do this? What happens in families to create the right kind of culture? For the purposes of this book, I will tailor my advice to parents struggling with kids who are abusing or recovering from addiction to substances. But the frameworks that I offer can actually be applied to *any* family with a child in *any* form of crisis.

Now that you know the big idea behind this book, I'd like to return to the frameworks that I mentioned earlier. There are three of them, and each one spotlights a key aspect of family culture. These frameworks are about

- emotional objectivity
- leadership
- conceptual knowledge

These three frameworks correspond in turn with three major dimensions of our personal experience:

- Emotional objectivity is what will allow you, the parent, to be consistent. It will make sure you don't run out of fuel on this journey. Maintaining emotional objectivity allows for successful parenting. Without it, no amount of "parenting tips" will help. I explore this framework in part 1.
- Leadership is about behavior—specifically, what you *do* to create a positive culture in your home. This section is more practical and will restore confidence in your decision making. This is the subject of part 2.
- Conceptual knowledge includes a practical understanding of child development, addiction, and mental

> health. This section is not just a basic review of diagnoses and medications. That kind of information is easily obtained elsewhere. What is harder to find is an explanation of the right approach to these topics for parents. You can use these concepts, which are discussed in part 3, to guide what you *think*.

These frameworks overlap in many ways, of course. Sometimes it's hard to separate them. But organizing the frameworks in this way can help you stay grounded when you're choosing what to do next for your child.

All three aspects of family culture are essential. However, this does not mean that you have to read the three parts of the book in their given order. Start at the point that speaks to your most pressing need or interest at the moment. If you're looking for ways to set more effective limits with your kids, for example, then start with part 2. If you have pressing questions about a mental health diagnosis, then begin with part 3.

Above all, I want you to get solid, easily remembered suggestions—ideas that you can take home and use, starting immediately. My goal is to keep things simple without being simplistic, and to give you frameworks that apply to any value system.

There are many books about screening your child for substance abuse problems. There are other books on how to engage your child in substance abuse treatment, and still others that deal with difficult children in general. In order to understand how this book fits into the existing literature, remember two things:

First, this book is for those parents who already know their child has a problem with drugs or alcohol, so I won't start from zero on this subject. However, many parents go through the process of discovery and the initiation of treatment only to wonder about how they should approach their child from that point on. If Johnny is two months out of rehab and starts copping an attitude in the kitchen, how much of this is related to his struggles for sobriety? How much of it is due to his ADHD (attention deficit/hyperactivity disorder)? And how much of it is just Johnny being a teenager? This is the kind of real problem that families face on a daily basis as they support a young person's recovery. These are the kinds of questions that I'll tackle.

Second, as mentioned earlier, the basic principles in this book are widely applicable. Of course, this book will speak intimately to parents with a child in treatment for addiction. But the ideas presented here will also apply to parents who are struggling with a wide range of other issues at home—rebellious kids, kids who have mental health problems, and much more. In addition, clinicians will find the frameworks easy to translate to a variety of clients.

I am trained as an academic. I am an advocate for scientific research and a consumer of medical journals. As such, I think like an academic and a researcher.

However, I do not function primarily in either of those roles in my daily work. In this book, you'll get suggestions that are not found in the pages of medical journals. That's because parenting is both commonsense and counterintuitive. It is both a science and an art.

For this reason, my goal is to talk about the often-abstract findings of researchers in ways that are consistent with the data—and to translate those findings into suggestions that parents can use.

I am fond of metaphors and analogies because I find them useful when communicating about subjects that are often emotionally laden. By taking the essence of a heavily sensitive topic and applying it in a scenario more benign, we can sometimes see the truth.

I wrote this book in a conversational tone because I want you to be able to hear my words as if we were in the same room, talking to each other face-to-face. Even more, I want to emphasize that you can be a tremendous force for good in your child's life, even if your family is in crisis right now.

In any case, the ideas in this book have been tested time and again in my own work with parents and their children. What you'll get in these pages is not an untested philosophy or a collection of provocative but empty musings. If you want to understand how addiction and mental health issues operate in young people—and what to do about them—then this book is for you.

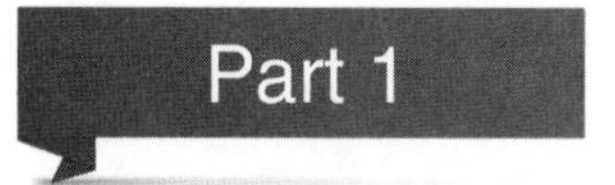

Frameworks for Emotional Objectivity

Chapter 1

The Pendulum and the Case for Emotional Objectivity

See if the following scenario applies to you.

You discover your child has an addiction. Finding drug paraphernalia in the child's bedroom, you see red. Feeling anger and panic, you let your emotions get the best of you in the moment. The next conversation with your child gets heated. There's a confrontation, and you say a few things you don't mean.

Now fast-forward a couple of weeks. Your child has just started outpatient treatment for addiction. At first, things appear to be going well. In response to her initial commitment, you decide to give her a chance. Secretly, you are also compelled by feelings of guilt for the things you said during the earlier confrontation. Partly to reward progress, but equally fueled by a need to settle your conscience, you decide to give your child an opportunity to earn your trust, allowing her to spend a weekend with "sober" friends.

On the following Monday, you discover that your child has relapsed. You feel betrayed on a personal level. You took a chance, and your child blew it. Conversations lose focus, and you find your emotions getting the best of you once again. Your spouse tells you one evening that, though you were right in your convictions, perhaps your delivery was too harsh.

Now, through the murky lens of conflicted emotions, it's hard to think objectively about the next steps. When will your child earn another opportunity for freedom? At what cost? And are you making the problem worse?

Many parents who struggle with addiction in the family have experienced this very chain of events. To put those events in a larger framework, remember that decision making in parenting often resembles a swinging pendulum. The best and most emotionally objective decisions are made when the pendulum is at midpoint. The extreme decisions on either side of this midpoint are driven by unbalanced feelings.

Pendulums do not stop midway once they gather momentum. They just keep swinging over a full arc, moving from one extreme to the other. Likewise, parental decision making without emotional objectivity is just a series of overreactions that swing between extremes, one compensating for another.

Let's look at this process in greater detail.

For many parents, it begins with the desire to believe in their addicted or otherwise troubled children—in their innate humanism and goodness. Despite knowledge of ongoing addiction, we send them to school or college. We give them their cars. We provide them with financial assistance. And we trust their word that things will get better. The pendulum is now set on one extreme.

Unfortunately, addiction is a disease that prevails independently of our children's baseline moral compass. As such, the disease inevitably lets us down. Addicted young people relapse. They flunk out of school. There are legal charges, fights, unpaid credit card bills, and suspect relationships. The drug use continues.

Having gone the extra mile at great emotional expense, we react to such events with pain and anger. We feel personally wounded and intentionally betrayed. Reacting to the perceived maliciousness of their relapse, the other extreme is reached. We yell, criticize, blame, and threaten, our faces red and fists clenched. Our pendulum speeds with frightening force, swinging past the midline to the opposite extreme with no chance of coming to rest in the realm of emotional objectivity.

Eventually, our feelings of spite are replaced by regret and introspection: *It was the disease, not my child. I have gone too far.* We fear that our relationship with our child has taken an irreversible turn for the worse. We now feel that we are a part of the problem, driving our child away from us when we should be his primary support. Having shown strong emotions, we may conclude that we overreacted. Our inclination, then, is to rectify this wrong by giving him another chance.

Of course, it is human to feel regret as parents. Unbeknownst to us, however, in these seeds of remorse is a falsely righteous calibration that will replace our emotional objectivity with another round of second-guessing. The pendulum gathers momentum once more and swings in the other direction. Back and forth it goes, bleeding our emotional reserves with each tortured swing: You give your child a chance, she lets you down; when you come down on her, feelings get out of hand, and you overreact. Each action overcompensates for the previous one. Eventually, it becomes impossible to know if any of your parenting decisions are objective at all. *Am I rewarding behaviors properly or being permissive in an attempt to make up for previous guilt? Am I setting the right limits, or am I going overboard because of spite?*

If you are currently dealing with a child in crisis, there will be times when you second-guess your own decisions. This process is all the more difficult with the passage of time, when each new decision is laid on top of a pile of already circumspect decisions. Though not sufficient in and of itself, emotional objectivity is a necessity for sound parenting. Looking at our behaviors through its lens helps us make sure that what we have done and said is consistent with our purpose: to help recover our child.

Parental decisions in the context of a child's addiction must occur with a clear conscience and focus. This is the foundation of every suggestion that follows. The goal behind all of them is to keep the pendulum at midpoint as much as possible.

Many parents have heard about the importance of consistency in parenting, but few are told how to go about being consistent. Finding emotional objectivity is the key. Without it, parenting decisions in crisis become one semiconscious overcompensation after another.

Bottom line: *Emotional objectivity is the art of stopping the swing between emotional extremes. It is the foundation for clear decision making in crisis. Ask yourself these questions:*

- Have you ever felt personally offended by your child's addiction or relapse?
- Have you made emotionally charged decisions or statements during your child's struggles?
- Did any of those decisions or statements make you operate from a place of guilt in later interactions?

Chapter 2

Happiness—Is That All There Is?

A number of psychological studies indicate that people who have children are less happy than people who don't, using various quality-of-life measures. It should then follow that people will increasingly not want children. Contrary to that notion, when you ask these same "less-happy" parents if, given the chance to go back in time, they would choose to have kids again, they overwhelmingly say "yes!"

There's something important going on here. Why would people choose to be less happy? I am assuming the parents in the study aren't just being politically correct and saying what people expect them to say. It may be that our definition of happiness is flawed. Maybe there are different kinds of happy. Or, there might be something else motivating parents besides happiness, perhaps something more fundamentally important in their lives. Actually, I think all of those things are true.

If our civilization faded away and a future archaeologist studied our language and culture, I think they would find our definition of *happiness* rather interesting. That's because we use two very different implications for the word *happiness* interchangeably.

When people say they are happy, they might refer to a momentarily euphoric sensation. Or, they might mean a longer-term sense of contentment. Philosophically, these definitions are at odds. I find that people confuse themselves with their use of the word *happy* in much the same way that they incorrectly interchange the words *sad* and *depressed*, the former being a short-term emotion and the latter being more of a disease state and condition.

The problem is that we often define happiness as feeling good all or most of the time. Happiness means getting all our circumstances in place, just the way we want them, and having events unfold exactly according to our plans. This scenario would lead to euphoria and short-term pleasure. Happiness as defined in this way is overrated and untenable. For most of us, it is going to be a rare experience.

Okay, but then what are we trying to say when we use the word *happy*? Or, if short-term happiness is elusive and difficult to maintain, what is it that we really want?

I believe that long-term happiness, or contentment, is better served by the term *peace of mind*. And I also believe that "less-happy" parents say they would enthusiastically sign up for having children again because of the value of meaningful, reciprocated relationships—that infinite sense of connectedness to their children.

So, in my opinion, peace of mind and connectedness are the two fundamental things people desire most. There you have it, the meaning of life! Joking aside, take a moment and really think about the things you've pursued in your life, whether they be job security, friendships, or travel. Think about what you really want out of your child's treatment for addiction. I would argue that a good proportion of our pursuits have peace of mind and/or connectedness as a final goal.

Corporations know this well. I have never seen this more explicitly demonstrated than in a series of beer commercials. A couple sits in beach chairs, staring at the ocean waves with their backs turned toward the camera. There is a subtle yet palpable tension and chemistry between them. The beach is inviting and serene. The commercial is selling connectedness or a sense of belonging through the imagery of two mysterious and attractive people who appear to be in a relationship. It's also selling us peace of mind; many people would be happy to watch the waves roll in endlessly on a beautiful, breezy day. The delusional part is the suggestion that beer will make those dreams come true.

It's important for parents to remember what they are really going for when their children are in treatment for or early recovery from addiction. This is a time when both parents and kids struggle with happiness. After the kids are sober for a few weeks, families suddenly wonder: *Where's all the joy? Where's the spiritual awakening? Why aren't we happy?*

Parents wrestle with these questions a lot. I try to reframe the conversation and ground them in a different framework. Instead of *happiness*, I'd rather talk about moving toward *peace of mind.*

It's important to remember that peace of mind can still be present when you're experiencing a lot of tough emotions. In fact, peace of mind can even be had when things aren't going well. These might seem like strange statements. How can you be at peace when you're feeling anger, sadness, or fear about your child's behavior? How can you be at peace when your child is still using?

Peace of mind for parents with addicted children is all about being content with our efforts, regardless of the results. This is incredibly difficult to do when parents are facing a tragedy, but it can still come with time. This peace of mind comes from knowing that we did the best we could despite our imperfections. It comes from honoring our connections with our children by being emotionally objective and maintaining good boundaries. And it comes from realizing that, regardless of our efforts, our power to help is finite.

Let me illustrate this in another way:

Every parent gets a deck of cards to play in life. Each card represents a realistic possibility—an action that's within our power to take; an action that bears influence on our children.

Now, no parent ever plays these cards perfectly. Even if they did, this card game has no guarantee of victory. The cards are also limited in supply. Every parent I know plays the cards honestly. They all make mistakes, but their intentions are true and compassionate.

When parents are dealt a tragic hand, it is common for them to second-guess their sequence and strategy. This is usually highly unproductive and ruins their emotional objectivity. They must remember that the cards in the deck are all they get. Furthermore, even flawless parental execution and play cannot guarantee results.

When their child enters treatment for addiction, parents often wonder if they left some card unplayed: *Did something happen in our family that caused addiction? Should we have done something differently? Could we have prevented this?* They get lost in "woulda, coulda, shoulda," and that creates unnecessary anguish.

These questions—and the attendant suffering—arise when parents lack valid frameworks for assessing their child's issues. If you have useful frameworks for understanding children, addiction, and mental health, then you don't have to ask those questions so often. You save yourself a lot of misery. You also free up energy that you can then channel into effective parenting—being emotionally objective, acting as leaders in your home, and supporting the professionals who work with your child in treatment. In short, you gain peace of mind. *Helping you get there is the real purpose of this book.*

When it comes to addiction, I tell parents that they get more cards than anybody else in terms of their child's life. However, we are not omnipotent. We do not get an unlimited set of cards to play. For example, your deck doesn't include heredity. If your child inherited a vulnerability to addiction or a mental health condition, that is beyond your control. Heredity represents one set of cards that you don't get to play.

A lot of parents come to me when their child is in treatment and play the "if only" game: *If only we hadn't tried to toilet train him so early. If only we'd kept him at home instead of sending him to day care. If only we'd moved to a neighborhood with better schools. If only we hadn't gotten divorced.*

These parents are aspiring to a kind of perfection. They want to go back in time and replay their cards. I remind them of something that they already know—you can't start the game over. And, even if they had played all their cards perfectly, their child still might not have stayed sober or otherwise problem-free.

When their family is in crisis, parents behave like a sports team. A good team huddles together when they're falling behind, develops objective leadership, and goes back out on the field. A bad team falls apart in the locker room. People start pointing fingers and assessing blame: *You shouldn't have started in the first quarter. It's the coach's fault because he subbed me out too early. You didn't train hard enough.*

Family members can do this, too. Sometimes they point to an event in the past and trace the problems with their child to that specific point in time. *We really blew it then*, they say. And sometimes there's an element of blame: *You should have done that differently*. Perhaps parents abused or neglected their child at some point. Perhaps there were mixed messages about drugs. Perhaps they didn't set the best example with their own behaviors.

My job is to help families put a stop to these exchanges and say, "Okay, here's the new playbook. Now, how are we going to move forward as a team?"

Extreme situations, where a child experiences sexual abuse, physical abuse, or another form of trauma at the hand of a parent, are more difficult to mend. Saying, "That was all in the past, and now we're moving ahead," is not going to do the job. It may take a long time for the parents responsible for the trauma to feel completely absolved in their hearts; perhaps it will never happen. But if these parents learn to practice leadership and emotional objectivity, there will come a time in the future when they'll have an opportunity to make amends. I've seen this happen countless times. While it doesn't completely make up for the past trauma, it does bring everyone back to the present moment and place the responsibility for recovery back where it belongs—squarely on the child's shoulders.

I cannot guarantee that your child will stay sober or experience a life free of addiction or other mental health issues. But I can help you discover the peace of mind that comes from knowing, at the end of the day, that you helped your loved one as much as you possibly could.

When searching for explanations about what happens in our family, we naturally look at the past. And the past is incredibly valuable. History does repeat itself: Our history is the number one predictor of our future actions. Yet, we don't have to let the past turn into a ghost that haunts our peace of mind in the present.

Bottom line: *Peace of mind is knowing that you got a limited number of cards to play when you became a parent, and that you're playing those cards to the best of your current ability. Ask yourself these questions:*

- Have you punished yourself for making bad decisions with your child in the past? If so, how has that affected your emotional objectivity?
- Have you blamed yourself or another family member for contributing to your child's addiction? Even if the accusations were accurate, did you find that this was helpful?
- Does something from the past blur your approach to your addicted child?
- Are your expectations for what *you* can do about your child's addiction realistic?

Chapter 3

The Roles We Play for One Another

When I'm at work, I play the role of a physician. Every once in a while—and maybe not as often as I'd like—people listen to me when I give advice on medical stuff.

Whenever I see my mother, however, it's a completely different story.

My mother believes everything she reads in Korean newspapers about health care, weird diets and all. I believe that this goes all the way back to my childhood and the kooky advice found through her church friends, traditional herbalists, and local Korean publications. Like the children of many Asian mothers, I grew up drowning in a deluge of well-intentioned and unnecessary tips for health. There were times when she made me drink strange teas every morning and prohibited me from eating anything that I actually liked.

One drink I'll never forget was a combination of a raw egg and honey and some other ingredients, the memory of which I have tried to suppress due to trauma. Then there was another brown liquid that was filtered and tasted like mulch and mothballs. I had to consume this concoction because she feared I was too skinny as a child.

As I went through my medical training, I confirmed that many of my mother's tips were overblown and sometimes hilarious in their inaccuracy. Still, I loved her all the same.

Now that she is getting older, the tables have turned. I find myself giving her medical advice during holidays and family visits. My advice is about blood pressure and cholesterol, standard stuff, and I make sure to give my academic sources.

Despite my attempts, I must admit that, to date, she hasn't listened to a word I've said. She nods and smiles, then counters with, "I read in the Korean newspaper that..." to which I always catch myself getting flustered. We then just stare at each other and laugh. I laugh because the situation is ridiculous, but also because I understand. I'm not sure why she's laughing.

To my mother, my role will always be that of a son, not a physician. And I suppose, to be fair, my mother was never a health expert in my eyes, either.

So it is with families sometimes. The point of this scenario is that we can have the best arguments, the most meaningful messages, the most thought-provoking insights, and we still may be tuned out by those we love. Even if we have great advice to give, it will only be accepted when we are in the right role to deliver said advice.

Family members often ask me about what role they should play in a loved one's recovery. How much should they help? What kind of talks should they have? Should they remind their children of therapeutic lessons or go over relapse prevention skills? My usual reply is simple: *First, play the role you already have.* Mothers need to be mothers, grandparents need to be grandparents, and so on. Where a child in recovery is concerned, living out that role in an impeccable way is enough for us to do.

Our intuitions as parents sometimes lead us astray in times of crisis. There isn't anything we wouldn't do for our children. At an instinctive level, some of us want to stop eating and sleeping and dedicate every second of our time to recovering our child. However, the reality with another person's addiction is that the best any of us can do is to hold open the door to recovery, provide support, deliver the best pep talk, and cheer. In the end, it is the addicted person's decision to walk through that door.

It's tempting for family members to take on extra roles to support their children. Sometimes this is unavoidable. Parents routinely schedule appointments for their children or find resources for help. Nothing wrong there. Pursue this path unchecked for too long, however, and most parents find that they are doing all the work in treatment while their children remain stuck. If they aren't careful, soon they are operating as co-therapists, parole officers, confidants, and everything in between. Each stretch of our primary role may appear justified, but as a whole, these stretches undermine our emotional objectivity. This is simply unsustainable. The multiplicity of roles can be particularly hard to avoid if you are a teacher, therapist, or health care professional, or are in any other profession that offers general insights about your child's condition.

Here is an example.

Young people in treatment recognize the need to be away from their immediate home environment in order to stay clean and sober. This often means getting away from using friends, dealers, and other triggers to start using again. But sometimes they choose to pursue their recovery under the supervision of a family member—a grandparent, uncle, aunt, or older sibling.

There are many times when such arrangements may be of clear benefit, but I would advise some caution in condoning such decisions. It's one thing to provide a safe place for a relative to recover. It's another thing completely to police that person's treatment.

Let's say you are an aunt, and your niece wants to move in with you after residential care. What other supports are available? Does she have mental health needs? If she is in a Twelve Step program, are her meetings and sponsors within reach? What will happen if she relapses? Will you hold resentments or take it personally? Will her immediate family members hold you accountable?

I care deeply for the young people under my care. But my role is clinical. I cannot become their best friend or replace their family. There are clear lines that help me maintain objectivity and compassion.

Looking at it that way, it's easy to see why roles are important in families as well. Once we know what we can and cannot do for our loved ones, the less resentment we'll hold, and the more supportive we can be.

Bottom line: *Don't try to copilot your child's treatment program. Just be a parent. Ask yourself these questions:*

- How does your role in your child's recovery differ from that of your child's doctor, therapist, or other treatment providers?
- What specific behaviors on your part might indicate that you're trying to take on someone else's role?

Chapter 4

You're Not the Buddha—Understanding Your Emotions

Despite all my training and education, and despite the fact that I live and breathe my work with adolescents and young adults on a daily basis, I have quickly realized that I have substantial limitations as a parent. (And as of this writing, my son is not even a year old.)

To be frank, I always knew that this was the case. I have never subscribed to the delusion that my professional specialty and expertise would somehow lend me a distinct advantage in parenting. As we engage in a dialogue about frameworks for parenting troubled adolescents, I want to make sure we are jumping into this together with eyes wide open, well aware of our collective strengths and deficits as role models.

Begin with the fact that we all have emotions. Emotions vary in intensity and in degree of political correctness. But, in reality, no emotion is "wrong." If anything, they are our most sincere calling cards. There's no need to suppress your emotions in the service of living up to some vague idea of stoic neutrality. You're not the Buddha (and neither am I). So why pretend to be? This book is about emotional objectivity for the rest of us.

To understand the role of emotions further, let's examine the dichotomy between our true emotional nature and society's expectations for how we should feel. The road to recovery is a marathon and not a sprint. There are triumphs and failures. At some point in what can be an exhausting treatment journey, even the most vigilant parents can experience rage, bitterness, betrayal, and even the desire to give up on their child.

Many parents feel guilty about such emotions, and our society certainly lacks a forum for openly discussing such perceived "insensitivity." We are bombarded with media images that depict Hallmark moments and send strong messages about how we are supposed to feel. Movies depict picture-perfect holidays—people walking off into the sunset, holding hands with full understanding and acceptance of one another, and smiling ad nauseam.

If only our relationships were actually so simple.

Parents place tremendous expectations on themselves when their child struggles with addiction. Their precious child is in need. In response, they must give advice, remain calm, and scrutinize. They must rally and protect and sacrifice, all in one gesture. Parents channel literary, media, and archetypal images for inspiration: Mother Teresa, Gandhi, Buddha, even fictional characters. And with the intention of imitating these lofty people, parents suppress their politically incorrect emotions, like anger, hatred, and hopelessness.

But most of us are not superhuman or saintly. Nor do we need to be in order to help our loved ones.

In my experience, the truth is that *parents who are in denial of their full emotional range are more likely to burn out or lash out*. Later chapters will detail the mechanisms of this process. But for now, we simply need to admit that we sometimes have feelings that aren't ideal. After all, feelings aren't true or false. Whether they are petty or noble, feelings are the most honest parts of ourselves.

I am not asking you to succumb to negative feelings, only to be realistic about who you are and what you experience. I'll provide a framework for this with a little self-disclosure.

My father was ill for many years before he passed away. I

knew his condition would slowly lead to his death. He went blind in one eye and then the other. His kidneys failed, and his organs slowly shut down. I was in medical school when he first had major complications. I recall the emotional turmoil and the feelings of despair and helplessness. I knew what was going on, but I also knew there was little anyone could do.

Over the next few years, my father suffered, and so did the rest of the family. Empathy, compassion, and concern for his welfare were paramount, but other emotions nagged as well.

I recall shuddering every time my mother called me while I was in residency, anticipating another setback in my father's condition. Seemingly petty feelings and thoughts ran through my mind as time passed—thoughts that I am not proud of, but thoughts that were real. For example, I thought about my father passing away sooner rather than later and the impact that would have on him and on us. Would he suffer less? Would we? Though I entertained these thoughts for but a moment, I felt intense shame for having them. Being a physician only exacerbated this shame. I tried my best to be all things for my family at the time, but this made me feel even more like a hypocrite.

Later, and before my father passed, I came across research on caretakers, including family members who took care of their sick loved ones. The research was brutally honest about the psychological distress caretakers faced and about the limited resources available to them. I found the research validating. I started to give myself permission to be fallible. I didn't deny what I thought were inappropriate feelings, but gave them audience and processed them so they wouldn't take over.

By the end, I reached a certain peace with my father's condition and, interestingly, with him. I grieved his death, but felt fortunate to be free of any lingering conflict. To this day, I consider it a blessing to have said all I needed to say to him, and to have been supportive—imperfectly so, but to the best of my capabilities.

Parenting a young person with addiction requires tapping

into strengths and reserves parents don't know they have. Paradoxically, being an effective parent also means fully acknowledging all of your emotions—even the "bad" ones. With that permission comes the wisdom and strength to act wisely, no matter what you feel.

A big part of the art and science of emotional objectivity is remembering that you're not a Zen master. You're not a stoic philosopher. You're not a saint. Best of all, you don't have to be. So quit trying to be one.

Bottom line: *When we place unfair expectations on ourselves about what we should feel versus what we actually feel, we are bound for failure. Ask yourself these questions:*

- Have you felt ashamed about entertaining negative thoughts about your child's addiction? If so, how did you deal with them?
- Did those thoughts influence your emotional objectivity?
- Is there a way that you can acknowledge a wide range of emotions about your child's addiction on a daily basis (hopeful and pessimistic, blaming and forgiving, and so on) so that you remain more objective on the whole?

Chapter 5

A Fortune Cookie a Day; or, Emotions Matter More Than Logic

When I was in college, I was a dashing, long-haired philosophy major. (The long-haired part is important for visual imagery; the dashing part is my retrospective wishful thinking.) Anyhow, I worshipped at the altar of reasoning and logic. I took abstruse classes like epistemology, which is the science of figuring out what we actually know. I felt that every problem in life could be solved by finding the right formula, the correct rationale.

In my career in medicine, I have come to find out that there are realities for which there is no convenient universal logic, no unifying theory. I slowly started to realize that emotions, and not logic, drive most of our decision making, and that psychological underpinnings could shine a light into the logistical inconsistencies in our nature.

For example, most people see others as a mirror of themselves. What this means is that people see their own traits in others. This is why addicts can pick out other addicts, and girls with hidden eating disorders can spot other girls with the same problem. What follows is that we also assume other people think like us. An addicted young person who does not trust others might discover in therapy that he does not find himself to be trustworthy, hence a vigilant tendency to see untrustworthiness in others.

Sometimes conflicts arise because emotional undercurrents are felt but not acknowledged. This is partly the reason that political discussions get so heated. Both sides of a political issue have ideologies that may be logically sound on some level. Tensions ensue, however, not because of the logic, but because of the implied emotional statements that one party interprets from the other. One side might see the other as composed of thinly veiled elitists; their opponents might view them as people who cannot take accountability for their own life predicaments. All the platforms and party statements do little to convince opponents, because logic cannot get people on the same page emotionally.

Life is about emotions, not logic. If logic ruled the day, I would be out of a job and everyone would be problem free, reading a fortune cookie every morning and knowing exactly what to do. In the case of addiction, we'd educate people about their faulty logic and lead them to recovery with a 100 percent success rate.

Unfortunately, that's not the world we live in. *The mystery of life is not about figuring out what we should do; it's about why we don't do the things we know we should.*

Here we face a perennial problem for human beings, as demonstrated by the vast self-help literature about overcoming procrastination and following through on our goals.

When we deny that we are emotionally driven creatures at our core, we can start to live a double life, one where our ideas and our daily actions don't match up. For now, understand that your philosophies and ideas alone will not get the job done, not for you or your child. Don't get upset if your child cannot see your point of view. Understand that emotional undercurrents, no matter how seemingly illogical, drive your and your child's decision making at times. How many times have parents explained their sound rationale to their addicted loved one, only to be met with temporary understanding and eventual disappointment? Despite this truth, I see parents (especially fathers) rely on logical arguments as the default standby for dealing with their troubled children. A later chapter on teenage neurodevelopment will shed more light on this issue.

There are two ways that people can resolve a conflict. One way is to draw a line in the sand and play tug-of-war until someone gives. That can lead to victories, if you can call them that, but it rarely results in partnerships. The other is to walk across the line in the sand, put your arm around the other person, and gaze from his vantage point. Once he understands that you can see a situation from his perspective emotionally, he might be more inclined to come across the line and join you.

In more practical terms, I often advise parents to understand that their children are driven by emotions, especially in addiction. This does not mean parents should give ground on their home expectations. They can, however, learn how to give credence to their child's emotions, no matter how irrational, without compromising sound limit setting on their part.

I would advise practicing a couple of skills to accomplish this. They are reflective listening and validation. These are skills parents can use to improve emotional communication, but remember that I don't want you to be a therapist with your child. So use them with your "parent cap" on.

Reflective listening can be as simple as parroting your child's sentiments.

"Mom, I tried to talk to my teacher, but he wouldn't hear me out."

"Sounds like you feel unheard."

I know it sounds superficial, but try it. You'll find that your child will feel supported and will continue on with her emotional stream of consciousness. Notice that you aren't agreeing or disagreeing with her, just reflecting. When you use reflective listening, refrain from inserting advice into the reflective statements, as that will appear manipulative.

If you want to be savvier, try to summarize what your child is saying to let her know you understand.

"My boyfriend is mad at me, I'm losing my friends, and I had an argument with my drug counselor."

"Wow, sounds like you are having a bad day. Lots of things going on at once."

The second skill is validation, and it simply builds on reflective listening. Validation means you can walk in your child's shoes emotionally and show her that you understand why she might feel a certain way. Again, you might not agree with her conclusions or decisions, but that does not need to be stated explicitly. Validation requires more than verbal parroting. Your facial expressions, body language, and tone of voice should reflect support unequivocally.

For example, if a young child doesn't want to go to school one day, you might validate his feelings while maintaining your expectations. "I really know it can be tough to go to school sometimes, AND you still have to go." We all have days when we don't want to go to work or do something else. We aren't always looking for a way out, either. Sometimes we just need someone to understand that it isn't so easy. If your child doesn't want to participate in substance abuse treatment, you can respond with, "I know the changes required in treatment can be hard to deal with" (pause, let this sink in, and show supportive body language and facial expressions). You'll be surprised that you can support your child's feelings 100 percent without giving ground on your expectations for him. Though addictive behaviors are unpredictable, parents often have more success with validation than "devastating" logical arguments. Once people feel heard, they are more willing to surrender a confrontational stance.

Bottom line: *For now, surrender your reliance on intellect as a foundation for your child's recovery. Ask yourself these questions:*

- During a discussion or argument, have you ever tried to reason with your child about becoming sober, only to have her ignore your advice in the moment or later?
- How did you react when she could not see your logic?
- How could you have approached the conversation differently using validation as a tool?

Chapter 6

Checking In with Your Emotions Is Like Taking Out the Trash

If you don't take out the trash on a regular basis, it begins to build up. It begins to smell. And when you finally do summon the courage to haul it outside to the garbage can, the task really stinks, and juices are leaking out of the bag.

Needless to say, this experience does not give you an incentive to take out the trash the next time. In fact, you're more likely to think, *Thank God I'm done with* that. *Yuck! I'm never dealing with that again.*

Some people are like this with feelings. They never want to deal with the negative ones. Their negative feelings pile up like trash. Every once in a while, they walk around their internal homes and smell something awful, but they never acknowledge the full extent of their garbage piles: anger, resentments, politically incorrect thoughts, and feelings of inadequacy. Ignoring the smells does not make the trash go away. Other people notice the smell as well, believe me. Eventually, their emotional garbage has piled up so much that it starts to flow out the windows and leak into other rooms. They are finally forced to "take the trash out" by dealing with their emotions, but the experience is overwhelming. They break down and cry, or scream in a rage. They are unnerved and frightened by their loss of control over their feelings. Once they have purged, they are discouraged from ever dealing with such feelings again, with their previous experience serving as a painful deterrent. So the trash pile starts to grow again.

A much more functional option is to deal with the trash on a regular basis, before it begins to fester and make you too uncomfortable. Take it outside. Give it some space. Give it some fresh air. It may not always be the most pleasant experience, but it's not as bad as dealing with a giant, decomposing pile. Then you can let it go and get on with your life.

I coach kids and parents to take out their internal trash—unpleasant emotions—every day. When you do this on a regular basis, life is much easier. Resentments and fear don't build up. They might return, but you'll know what to do with them. Negative feelings are less likely to get the best of you. Emotional explosions are less likely to happen down the road.

Taking out a piece of internal trash means three things:

1. *Give the emotion a name.* The first step to taking out the garbage is admitting that it exists. That bag truly is there, taking up space in your house and emitting its noxious aroma. Dealing with emotions is similar. Giving the emotion a name allows you to admit that it exists, and that's an important step.

   Taking this step means developing a vocabulary for your emotions. Emotions are like colors. Initially, we know basic feelings, like anger or sadness, that might equate with basic colors like red and blue. As we get older, we learn about more subtle shades of colors in much the same way that we learn about feelings. Feelings come in infinite mixtures, with complicated nuances. It isn't just *I'm angry my daughter relapsed.* It's more like *I feel upset about my daughter's relapse. A part of me feels like she's holding our family hostage, and another part of me feels like I've let her down even though I know I haven't. I feel numb and shocked and helpless and cynical and guilty all at once.*

There are many simple exercises that you can use to expand your emotional vocabulary. For one, just search the Internet for *feeling words*. You'll find lots of charts and long lists of words. Pick one and dig into it a little. See if it captures what you are experiencing. Expanding your feeling vocabulary can help you make finer distinctions between emotions and increase your self-awareness. Greater awareness makes for greater emotional objectivity.

2. *Give the emotion space*. After taking the trash bag out of your house and tossing it in your garbage receptacle, you might benefit from just standing there, putting your hands on your hips, and staring at it for a few seconds. You've just gotten a firsthand experience of the power of taking out the trash. It's a lesson worth savoring. It can also be a time for reflection.

   You can use a similar process with emotions. After admitting that you're feeling an emotion and giving it a name, allow yourself to sink into it for a few moments. Let yourself fully experience it. Remember, emotions don't occur in a vacuum. They are interconnected with our thoughts and behaviors. It's therefore important to note what comes before, during, and after an emotional experience.

   One way to do this is to collect "data points" about the emotion. Collecting data points allows you to step back from an emotion, give it some space, and examine it in an objective way. You're like a scientist who's making observations. You're just collecting data. You notice how an emotion affects you, and you also notice how it is linked to other behaviors, thoughts, and subsequent emotions.

For example, see if you can notice where an emotion registers in your body. Does it show up as tightness in your stomach? When feeling upset, do you hold your breath or take more shallow breaths? When you are anxious, do you feel fatigued or get a headache? Those are data points.

You might notice that you act a certain way when you are avoiding a feeling, or that you behave and think in a predictable pattern when you feel something. Do certain emotions start a cascade of reactions you didn't realize before? For example, do you get short with those around you when you are worried? Those are data points, too.

You can collect data points about your thinking. Emotions can trigger lines of thought such as *This really sucks. There's no way that I should have to put up with this. People should never act this way.* They can conjure memories of times the emotion was felt before. *This feeling reminds me of my father's relapse with alcoholism.*

Don't make judgments about yourself, and instead observe the feeling and its impact in much the same way that you might observe the ripples in the water after tossing a rock in a lake. When treated this way (and it takes practice), even the worst emotions start to lose their grip on us.

3. *Give the emotion an audience.* Now give your emotions some "air time." Voice your emotions. Give them life. This is the most important step. Find people whom you trust—your spouse, partner, or another trusted relative or friend. Choose someone who knows when to be quiet, how to listen without judgment, and how to keep things confidential. Tell

> this person what's going on inside you, and do it on a regular basis. This can give you a tremendous sense of relief.
>
> There have been a few occasions when I have cried during speeches and presentations. The sentiments are usually about my commitment to helping kids and my understanding of their need for advocacy. I have cried about the feelings I've had when working with families in inner-city Baltimore, for example. These are feelings I know well in my heart and my mind, but when I voice them, they come to life, and I am surprisingly bursting with raw emotion, almost as if I had just felt them for the first time. It is a little embarrassing, to tell the truth, but the point is that being aware of a feeling or thought internally and voicing it externally are completely different things.
>
> When young people share the depths of their addictive experiences at Hazelden, they are initially resistant. "Why do I have to share my story again? I already know." The same goes for parents when they come to our parent program: "Our kids know how much their use has affected us." Parents and kids are often surprised to find out how powerful the experience of voicing well-versed sentiment is when it is expressed honestly, vulnerably, and with conviction. Within such cathartic moments are the seeds of change.

Taking out the trash is one way to process our emotions. Processing is different from venting. Venting is just letting out a frustration. Venting in and of itself is not that therapeutic; sometimes it just gets parents more wound up or feeling self-righteous in their stance. Processing is expressing the feeling, taking ownership of it, and learning how to put it in its place.

When you're willing to do these three things, then you can process even the most unpleasant emotions without leaving a harmful residue. Then you can choose your behaviors with a more spacious perspective and a clearer head.

Again, there's no big revelation here. You already know about the value of admitting your emotions and talking about them. But how often do you *act* on what you know? How often do you voice what is inside your heart? A big part of emotional objectivity is taking the actions that seem obvious and putting them into consistent practice.

By the way, you can apply the above three steps to any emotion, pleasant or unpleasant. It's important to fully admit and experience emotions such as fear, anger, and sadness. And, you can also deepen your experience of joy by naming it, giving it space, and giving it an audience.

Finally, I would strongly recommend that parents look into getting an individual or family therapist of their own. Getting involved in your child's addiction treatment directly is definitely a requisite, but you may find that too much involvement on your part creates a conflict of interest for the therapist. You might find yourself wondering, *Is this my therapist or my child's?*

Bottom line: *A big part of emotional objectivity is being willing to admit, fully experience, and share what you're feeling. With knowledge and permission come the wisdom and strength to act wisely, no matter what you feel. Ask yourself these questions:*

- When feeling a strong emotion, how do you habitually respond? Does it start a cascade of thoughts, feelings, and behaviors that you aren't aware of?
- What are you feeling right now? If some emotion is present, give it a name and describe how it shows up in

your body and in your mind. Then give it a voice and see if it makes you feel different.

- When was the last time you talked to someone at length about your emotions?
- Do you have support to help you process your emotions? If not, how could you secure such support?

Chapter 7

One Dollar a Day—
Your Emotional Budget

When it comes to the early phase of recovery, we have quite a few expectations for our children, and justifiably so. We have seen them slip so far developmentally, in social, academic, and personal domains. There is a pressing need to fix their attitudes, their friends, their grades, their relationships, and their daily disciplines. All of these are pressing issues, but fighting a battle on multiple fronts to enforce every single expectation at all times can wear parents out, eventually eroding their emotional objectivity.

Parenting is about managing capital—emotional capital. And you have only a limited amount of that.

Imagine that you start every day with one dollar's worth of emotional capital to spend on your child. Every time you have to enforce an expectation for your child, you "spend" part of that capital.

Here's the potential problem: If you spend seventy cents of your dollar in conflicts with your child about brushing teeth and eating breakfast, then you've got only thirty cents left to spend later in the day on other issues. Depending on the day, these can include anything from getting homework done to making sure that your child hangs out with kids you can trust.

One dollar per day doesn't sound like much. And of course,

this is just a metaphor. The point is this: Your emotional capital is not infinite. Far from it. If you just imagine that it adds up to a modest, fixed quantity—such as a dollar—you're more likely to spend that capital wisely.

When parents forget about having just one dollar per day, there are usually a couple of things going on. First, they genuinely want to accomplish many things with their kids. They want to make sure that every question gets answered, that every problem gets solved: Stop drinking alcohol, stop smoking cigarettes, do well in school, clean your room, be nice to your sister—and, while you're at it, get a haircut! And, parents think that they're giving ground if they don't get all this done at once.

This is kind of a neurotic tendency, and I don't mean that in a negative way. Neuroticism is a fundamental personality trait; it refers to a tendency to feel distressed or anxious quickly. Good parents and good physicians are neurotic to some degree. We check and worry even when the threats to our families are not considered imminent. This kind of vigilant alarm system can be really helpful at times. However, truly skilled parents know how to keep this personality trait in check so that it doesn't color their entire relationship with their child.

It's better, from the standpoint of emotional objectivity, to make a list of priorities—things that you want your child to accomplish. Take these large outcomes and translate them into small actions that you and your child can do on a daily basis. Maybe you start with prioritizing larger expectations like staying sober and getting back in line with school. These are nonnegotiable. Attitude is important, too, but as long as he is respectful, you give him some slack, knowing that the change he is undertaking isn't easy. Your expectations haven't changed. This is not compromising. This is about expecting progress, not perfection. You don't have to tackle every issue with your child at once.

It's pretty simple, really—simple, but not easy.

Bottom line: *Don't tackle all of the issues with your child all at once. Ask yourself these questions:*

- Did you ever feel the need to go a hundred miles per hour and fix all of your child's issues at once?
- Did you ever expend your parental capital to such an extent that your child started to tune you out?
- Of all the changes you want in your child, which are the most important?

Chapter 8

The Difference between Knowing and Accepting

If you look up the words *know* and *accept* in a dictionary, you'll find that the first few definitions of those words are similar. For example, the Merriam-Webster online dictionary defines *know* as the ability to "perceive directly" and to "have direct cognition of" an event. Likewise, *accept* means being able to "receive willingly" and to "recognize as true."

If you scroll down a few lines, however, the definition of *accept* expands in a revealing way. To *accept* means "to make a favorable response" to an event—"to agree to undertake (a responsibility)."

When it comes to emotional objectivity, this is something that we really need to emphasize. Accepting means far more than just knowing the facts. Knowing is necessary, but not sufficient for effective change. Accepting comes with a duty to act on what you know.

Let's say that I am on a journey and I know there is a wall directly ahead of me. Knowing that the wall is there may not prevent me from running into it. After all, my knowledge does not necessarily compel me to do anything differently. But if I accept that the wall is there, then I make a right turn at the wall. By accepting the presence of the wall, I have changed my course accordingly. There is a "duty" I now have, based on my acceptance, that requires action. To bring the analogy closer to home, think about the difference between knowing that you have a medical illness versus accepting that medical illness (such as diabetes). What would that mean?

In these cases, the distinction between knowing and accepting seems obvious. But when it comes to a complex challenge like addiction, this distinction is easy to forget. When families enter treatment for substance abuse problems, many parents and kids know they have a problem but do not accept the changes and sacrifices required. Their lives are disrupted. They're in pain. But they cling to maladaptive beliefs and behaviors, the same ones that got them into treatment in the first place.

On the other extreme, addicts sometimes mistake acceptance for resignation. "I have a potentially fatal disease. I might as well give up." The difference between acceptance and resignation is that acceptance embraces the duty that comes with choices, whereas resignation implies a surrendering of choice.

Many children enter treatment with a desire to get better. Their intentions are actually quite sincere. When it comes to actually reinventing the mechanism of their addiction, however, they resist change at every turn. Whether it's their relationships, socialization preferences, stress coping techniques, or increased personal accountability, it can take considerable time and effort to create movement.

It's the difference between wanting to get in shape versus actually getting up to go to the gym every morning. Many out-of-shape individuals have a sincere desire to get in shape. But they do not accept the sacrifices required. It's the difference between wanting to reduce spending versus actually making budget cuts ("No, not my iPhone!"). The intentions in both cases are noble but are not sufficient.

There is a famous saying that insanity is defined as doing the same thing over and over and expecting different results. In the Big Book of Alcoholics Anonymous, the author reminds us that an alcoholic "will be *absolutely unable to stop drinking on the basis of self-knowledge*."[1] Admitting the fact of addiction is the subject of Step One. It is followed by eleven additional Steps that lay out a detailed program for changing the alcoholic's entire life. Taking all those Steps is where acceptance comes into play. This is supported by psychiatric literature, which clearly shows that insight alone does not lead to change.

The fact of your child's addiction means that the parameters of your family life have changed. The rules of engagement are now completely different. Acceptance of addiction calls for change on everyone's part. Your child now has a duty to work a program of recovery. She has to reexamine her relationships and her values, and have the courage to make an honest self-appraisal. And you have a duty to change in ways that will support this new life for your child. Your expectations and goals for your child, along with your perceptions of your family, have to be reexamined as well. For example, you might have spent years preparing for your child's transition to a college or prep school of choice. Those dreams can still be attained with successful treatment, but marching along a rigid timeline without accounting for the impact of addiction might lead to heartache. You and your child are now on a parallel journey of acceptance.

While knowing is an intellectual process, acceptance goes much deeper. Acceptance involves our emotions and our capacity to act. Acceptance engages our full humanity and touches the depth of our being.

Bottom line: *Accepting the fact of your child's addiction comes with a willingness to change what you do as a parent. Ask yourself these questions:*

1. *Alcoholics Anonymous*, 4th ed. (New York: AA World Services, 2001), 39.

- If you accept that your child has an addiction, what does that mean? What duty to change does that create for you?
- Have you reevaluated your and your family's priorities in the context of addiction?
- Are there some old beliefs or goals or perceptions about your child and your family that are hard to let go of? Talk to someone you trust about what those are.

Chapter 9

"I Told You Not to Put Ketchup on My Fries"—the Importance of Setting Boundaries

If you've had previous experience with therapy for yourself or your child, you've heard the term *boundaries*. Clinicians may have asked you to be mindful of your boundaries with your child, your spouse, and your extended family members.

When I bring up the term *boundary* in session, parents and kids often nod intuitively. The concept of interpersonal boundaries seems so obvious. Yet, when I ask them to define what boundaries mean for them, many have a hard time finding the right concept.

So what are boundaries in relationships, exactly?

Well, to explain, I must digress once more.

There is a philosophy called *pragmatism*. Pragmatism is the Forrest Gump of philosophies. It basically says that "stupid is as stupid does." Or, a thing is the sum of its effects.

Gravity, for example, is a concept best understood through pragmatism. People used to have a hard time conceptualizing gravity because science was at one time based on quantifiable observations made with our five senses. If you couldn't see, taste, touch, smell, or hear something, it was hard to capture it scientifically. Gravity, therefore, made little sense.

Pragmatists came around and simplified the discussion by

pointing out that gravity is just the sum of its effects. That is, gravity makes things fall to the ground. We enlightened modern folk understand gravity as a force, but the concept is still elusive in the abstract. The point is that some things are better defined by what they do and what impact they have.

This also applies to boundaries. To aid our definition, let me illustrate the pragmatic impact of boundaries.

Let's say you have a good friend. This friend is legitimately down on his luck, and his car broke down. He needs a ride to work, and he asks you for a favor. Being gracious and generous of heart, you offer to help out. Well, it turns out his workplace is an hour away from where you live. So, every day you spend an hour taking your friend to work and an hour picking him up later and returning him to his home. You're spending at least two hours of your day helping him.

This friend of yours is really in need, so you continue your service for a few days, then a week, then maybe longer. Soon you realize that you have a life of your own to live. You start to feel resentful.

Of course, having been raised as an upright individual by your parents, you feel guilty about this resentment. So you begrudgingly continue providing transport.

One day, you and your friend are hanging out eating burgers with some fries. Your friend attempts to fill a paper cup with communal ketchup but it goes all over your fries. Outraged, you yell, "I told you not to put ketchup on my fries!"

Your friend is stunned. He's never heard you yell before.

The question is: Were you really that upset about the ketchup? Or was it something else?

Obviously, you feel upset about the sacrifice you're making for your friend, and you also have ambivalent emotions about the help you're providing. What you must remember, however, is that the responsibility for not having set proper boundaries with your friend lies with you. If you'd known your limits for tolerating the burden of the additional two-hour daily commutes, you could have made that clear from the start. In the long run, your friend would have been appreciative. He wouldn't think you were "psycho" about french fries. And you wouldn't feel so guilty about yelling at a friend who's in need.

The above scenario demonstrates what boundaries are by looking at their effects. Basically, *you know boundaries are violated whenever you cannot sustain an act or thought or feeling—no matter how generous or humane.* This does not mean that we should all be individual isolationists and offer little in the way of altruistic service to anyone else. It does mean that we should actively think about what our limits are. And only we know where our limits exist.

Think about this for a second. The basic reasoning is parallel to making sound decisions in other areas of our lives. For example, we should lend money to others only if we are prepared for the possibility that we won't see it return. And people who are risk averse should not invest wildly in the stock market. The goal, in any case, is to minimize the "ketchup and fries" moments in our lives.

Bottom line: *To stay within our emotional boundaries, we should try to act in a way with others that limits our potential for regret. Ask yourself these questions:*

- Do you currently feel resentment toward anyone, including members of your family?
- If the answer is yes, did that resentment come to pass in part because of a lack of boundaries?
- Do you see a potential for boundary violations in any of your current relationships, even if you currently don't feel any resentment or regret about them?
- Think about your current role in your child's recovery. Is it sustainable? If it is not, will you grow to resent it?

Chapter 10

Codependency, Dependency, Trees, and Vines

Since we are on the topic of boundaries and roles in relationships, we need to mention two terms that are frequently thrown around in addiction treatment. The first is *dependency*, as in *dependent personality disorder*; and the second is *codependency*. Books are written about the topics of dependency and codependency alone, but here is a synopsis of these concepts that can help you maintain your emotional objectivity effectively.

Young people often use these terms inaccurately in therapy. They say they are codependent when they are just dependent and vice versa. Many authors will debate over how to properly define these terms. This is my take, and it's geared toward younger people and families.

Some people have dependent personality traits. That means that they rarely feel comfortable on their own. They need others to make them feel secure. They do not feel they can control their feelings or accomplish their goals independently. The dependency can become malignant, as these people can have unfair expectations of others (sometimes angrily) or will act to avoid abandonment. People with dependent personality traits can have plenty of skill and aptitude; what they lack is a confidence in their abilities.

I tell young people that some people are trees and some

people are vines. The trees have strong roots and trunks. They can stand on their own. Vines, on the other hand, need something else (like a tree) to prop themselves up. Now, some level of dependency is normal in adolescence and young adulthood, as all young trees need some support.

Within the framework of addiction, kids can lose their sense of self-efficacy, a belief that they are competent enough to achieve their goals. In treatment, we help them realize that although they were powerless over their addiction, they are powerful overall in their lives. It's just a matter of letting go of what they can't really control to gain control in the bigger picture. Many kids who find sobriety find that they thought they were vines, but were actually trees all along—heavy trees that weren't easy for others to carry. Put more practically, I see young people all the time who are tied to relationships that they feel they cannot live without. A goal of treatment is to have them find more meaningful relationships with healthy boundaries, so that they realize and cultivate their independence. One of the major reasons for setting boundaries and minding roles as parents is to encourage growth along this theme.

At this point you might be saying, "Wait, that sounds like codependency." That's because codependency is a type of dependency. Codependents also need to have others in their lives to prop them up, but sometimes in ways that aren't readily apparent. Codependents need to be needed. An example might be a girl who continually picks up "stray dogs" as friends and significant others, meaning that she chooses people who have clear needs. She may take them on as projects. Some codependents are doormats or insecure caretakers and enablers. Others appear to be driven and goal-oriented saints from a distance because of their concern for others.

One common thread about codependents is that they focus on the needs of others while neglecting their own problems.

They can be legitimately helpful to others, but they do not take care of themselves. The key is in degree and proportion. All parents have had to forgo their own needs for the needs of their child. But to do so excessively can be quite harmful to the parent and the addicted child. There can also be a problem with letting go when the child starts the journey to recovery and the codependent parent is no longer "needed." It is not uncommon for some parent-child relationships to really sour once the child enters recovery. The parents will complain that they do not approve of their child's choice in sober friends or significant others, or that the child has thanklessly stopped communicating with them in recovery. What they don't mention is the loss and abandonment they feel when they are no longer the "go to" person for their child's problems.

One of the reasons therapists do not encourage the pursuit of serious relationships in early sobriety is because of dependency and codependency. I have seen a number of promising recovery attempts turn south because the addicts put all their eggs in the basket of a relationship that didn't turn out like they thought it would. From the parent-child perspective, working on boundaries and emotional objectivity will ensure that you are a part of the solution, and not an ongoing part of the problem.

Bottom line: *Maintaining emotional objectivity and proper boundaries can help you avoid codependent relationships with your child. Ask yourself these questions:*

- Do you believe your child is prone to dependent or codependent relationships?
- Have you felt that you need to be the central agent for your child's recovery?
- Do you have a hard time setting limits with your

child while continually advocating for her, at times unnecessarily?

- Are you taking time to take care of yourself or to address your own issues while your child needs help with addiction? What do you think is the right balance?

Frameworks for Leadership

Chapter 11

Your House Is Not a Democracy

Yes, I said it.

Your house is not a democracy.

I'd like to make a few points here to build my case.

Intelligence does not equal wisdom. Let's face it. Our children are bright. They know a lot about technology. They seem to grow up and mature faster with each passing generation. They are articulate and precocious. They engage with causes and political movements in a way that's inspiring. We are blown away when they make profound, logical statements. We want to believe in their maturity. We want to consult their opinions. We want to believe.

However, there is a big difference between wisdom and intelligence. Intelligence has to do with knowledge; wisdom confers sound judgment. Intelligence is dependent on no more than a combination of curiosity and access to information. Wisdom requires emotional maturity, experience, and the ability to suppress our impulses at appropriate times.

When your child is in crisis, you must resist the temptation to overestimate her maturity. You don't want to underestimate it, either, but the goal is to show your mettle by first being a parent.

Today, I see an increasingly disturbing trend of parenting children based on the child's intellectual development as opposed to emotional maturity. This is the single biggest error that parents make. We mistake articulate logical arguments for sound decision making in the face of pressure. Part 3 of this book, including the chapters on how our children's brains develop, will shed further light on why they can sound so smart without being too wise.

We are not their friends, and we don't have to be "cool." Parents who fall victim to equating wisdom with intelligence are also susceptible to the fallacy that they should be their child's "friend."

I think every parent at one time or another has fantasies about being a "cool" parent—someone who's in tune with her kids. Someone who can jam on the guitar with his kids and communicate the wisdom of his own youthful experience in a vivid way. Someone who can lead her kids in the right direction by being more like a friend or an older sibling. Someone who can just inspire his kids to do well without setting limits or expectations through love and wisdom and open-mindedness and all the other well-intentioned, but possibly misguided, values of the 1960s. Someone who offers freedom of choice to her children with the sentiment that they will, in the end, make the right decisions and appreciate your trust.

I bet there are parents out there who hold such fantasies as an ideal. And, if you ask me, theirs is a parenting style in which success relies primarily on luck and genetics.

If you are reading this book, I'm probably not describing you. And that is just fine. You might have friends whose children are doing well, and though they don't try to be patronizing, they sometimes impart advice on what they did with their kids to avoid all the strife you've experienced. They may not have the genetic loading or mental health history your family might have, though they attribute the absence of these more to their prescient wisdom than anything else. I know that sometimes you might want to punch these people in their smug faces, but I would advise you not to do that. In a way, you can't blame your friends. Like anyone else, they believe that they deserve the good fortune they have earned with little luck or help, and that what calamity falls upon them is completely random and undeserved.

You can be honest about your own history of alcohol and other drug use—and still maintain your leadership. Parents are often not sure how to go about disclosing their own history of drug use. And when they do, the messages are all too often mixed. I know this because I ask the kids in my office about what their parents are saying at home on this issue.

The mixed messaging occurs because parents

- have different viewpoints and don't get on the same page
- lose sight of the big objectives when they talk to their kids about drugs and alcohol
- try to show their children that they used responsibly
- get lost in their stories and try to be "cool"

Somewhere in this dialogue, the main point about staying away from drugs gets lost.

Remember that you do not have to reveal all the details of your past drug use, even if your children ask about them. The idea is to have an *appropriate* discussion about health care, not a shocking or melodramatic one. Again, this is not a platform for parents to talk about how cool they were during their teen and college years. Their kids might not be interested in knowing this. (And some parents really weren't *that* cool, anyway.)

This is a matter of keeping things in perspective. When parents talk about cancer, diabetes, or heart disease that runs across generations of a family, the subject is likely to be discussed in an open and matter-of-fact way. But when the conversation turns to a relative's mental health diagnosis or drug addiction, some parents get lost in morality plays. The narration gets mixed up with judgments about right and wrong, good and bad, lack of willpower, and personal failure. A stigma kicks in and the discussion shuts down. That's something to avoid.

As a parent, you are the greatest influence on your children's development, even if they don't openly admit this. Underneath all their bluster, your kids are paying close attention to what you say and do. Research pretty conclusively shows that kids are susceptible to all sorts of messaging from media, friends, parents, and other sources of influence. And at the same time, parents who are more ambiguous about their stance on drug use have kids who are more prone to use. It's that simple.

Sweat the small stuff, such as easy access to prescription drugs in your house. More specifically, know who has access to your medicine cabinet. I am baffled by how many parents drop the ball on this. They have a minor knee operation, for example, go to their primary care doctor, and get a prescription for thirty oxycodone pills. The pain is manageable with basic Tylenol after a week or so, and the rest of the medication just sits in the medicine cabinet, free for the taking. This is a real lapse in leadership.

To compound the problem, some parents think they're doing the right thing by holding on to whatever medication is left over and saving it for a rainy day when they're in pain. Lo and behold, what happens is that one of their child's friends comes to the house, takes five of those pills (leaving enough of them so you don't know that any have been taken), and sells them for twenty dollars a pill on the market. This transaction creates a powerful incentive for this kid to do the same thing again.

Worse yet, the child is with friends at a party away from home, and someone there overdoses on medication and dies. After asking some questions, the authorities find out that the pills came from one of the parents' medicine cabinets. This is a situation you never have to find yourself in.

Thinking about and acting on concerns like disposing of unused prescription drugs, keeping alcohol out of reach, and taking other preventative measures doesn't make you a tyrant, uncool, or an untrusting parent. It makes you a responsible leader of your household.

Bottom line: *If you can manage to be your child's friend as a sort of "icing on the cake," then go for it. Otherwise, stick to being a parent, remembering that the greater wisdom is yours. You won't be nearly as cool, but your kids will be safer. Ask yourself these questions:*

- What kinds of behaviors might signal that you've sacrificed leadership in the home for friendship with your children?
- What will you say to your children if they ask about your own history of drug use?
- How easy would it be for your kids or their friends to access alcohol or other drugs in your home?

Chapter 12

If Your House Is Not a Democracy, Then What Is It?

While democracy is not the ideal model for parental leadership, totalitarianism and dictatorship are not really effective alternative models. Your family isn't like that, and successful families aren't run that way.

Being a leader in your family is less like running a government and more like running an organization. You are the CEO of your organization, the captain of your ship, or whatever other metaphor you can think of that puts you in the role of a leader. Don't take this analogy too literally, however. Your children are not employees. The goal is simply for you to function as a leader, especially during family crises. And like any successful company or sports team, a successful family pulls together as a unit around strong leadership.

What does that mean on a day-to-day basis, and what skills do you need?

The big-picture answer is that leaders set the right kind of tone in their organizations. They shape the company culture. Let's discuss a few leadership principles to keep in mind as you forge your own family's culture.

Think "macro," not "micro." As parents, we are trained from our children's births to micromanage. We change diapers.

We manage bedtimes and feedings. We fix "ouchies." From the start, we are the ones who are trained to change. And this is a beautiful thing. However, when our children start to grow, we let them feed themselves and encourage self-soothing while remaining available when they cannot handle the circumstances. When our children reach adolescence, we must at one point or another shift gears into a "macromanagement" style by focusing on the bigger picture and increasing our children's sense of self-efficacy. Through this process, our children learn accountability and independence.

We may recognize the need for macromanagement, but the balance can be hard to find. What are our children ready to handle, and how much is too much to place on them? This book has plenty of advice on how to handle such a balance. Unfortunately, the truth is that whenever our children are in danger or in need, we revert to micromanaging techniques. So, as you think about leadership in the home, keep your sights set on macromanaging as much as possible.

As an effective CEO of your home, you act as a household "macromanager" rather than micromanager. You give your children clear expectations and goals to achieve. At the same time, you grant children an age-appropriate amount of flexibility in *how* to achieve those goals.

For example, you can reasonably expect a healthy ten-year-old child to do his chores before dinner. It might be taking out the trash or bathing the dog. You could micromanage in this situation, but it's better to save your capital. Why sweat the small stuff as long as your child meets your core expectation? As long as the job is done reasonably well and in a timely manner, does it matter how it got done? This is macromanagement, rather than micromanagement, and it's a way to avoid unnecessary conflict.

With this suggestion I'm speaking especially to parents whose kids develop complex challenges early on—for instance, heart abnormalities, insulin-dependent diabetes, learning disabilities, or mental health issues. Children like this can bring out our natural parenting instincts in a full-throttle way. By the time that these children move into adolescence, their parents are often used to functioning as daily advocates for their child's well-being—a role that involves a lot of micromanagement. These parents may have no concept of how to function in any other way.

I coach these parents to back off gradually and give up control in stages that are appropriate to their child's situation. They start by hovering over their child with arms wide open. Over time, they learn to cross their arms, watch the child from a distance, and say, "Here are our expectations for you. We'll let you know *what* to do, but *how* you do it is up to you."

The same principles apply when your child is striving for recovery. You might decide to help your child set up treatment and other appropriate measures, especially as she is trying to find her footing with treatment and early sobriety. As treatment moves along, think about what fair expectations are for her and what kind of things she should be doing on her own. For example, she may be able to keep track of her appointments or AA meetings, or set up a productive schedule that the two of you can agree on.

Share information on a need-to-know basis. A boss at work is not under obligation to reveal everything she knows to her employees. In fact, it may be quite detrimental for the boss to wear her emotions on her sleeve or to reveal her inner thought processes. For example, let's say the company is struggling one year. The boss has her share of doubts about the future, but she becomes hopeful about upcoming opportunities as the year proceeds.

Now, it's one thing for the boss to inform her workers about the big picture; it's another thing entirely to bare all of her emotions without a filter, or to feed speculation. That can affect morale and create useless concern within the organization.

Likewise, you want to exercise leadership by giving your

children information on a "need-to-know" basis. As a parent, you don't have to share all the details of your work-related problems and other adult-level stressors with your children. Since your home is not a democracy, not all of the members have to be fully informed.

A skilled CEO is under no obligation to immediately inform employees that he's considering a round of layoffs, for example, or that the company is being targeted for acquisition by a competitor. (You can't lay off your children, by the way; there is some clause about that in the human resources manual.) Likewise, you don't have to tell your children that you're worried about getting laid off next year or having a hard time putting away money for their college fund.

It's more important that you be a steady source of morale and direction on a daily basis. This is critical for business leaders, and it's critical for parent-leaders.

Please understand that I am not endorsing lying to your children. Nor am I suggesting that you shelter your kids from all knowledge of your life struggles. However, I am urging you to share information carefully—in ways that your children can absorb while still leaving your family leadership role intact.

Remember that, as CEO, you make the rules—and you can change them. As a general principle, avoid making promises to a child who's in treatment. It is important to take everything off the table. You don't want to deal with a comment such as "Dad, you promised I could go back to college right away if I did treatment!" I cannot tell you the number of conflicts that have risen from parents' "promising" something to a child in recovery. When that child struggles, the parents feel torn about backtracking on their promises, and children are very good at playing the hypocrisy card.

Explain to your children that you aren't perfect and that you (and your spouse or partner) have the right to change the structure if you see fit. After all, a CEO who made some miscalculations should be given the right to recalibrate.

Everything in the home is a privilege. As household CEO, you also know the difference between a right and a privilege. Despite what any teenager says, for example, owning a cell phone is a privilege, not a "right." And it's up to you whether to grant that right. Unless we remind kids of this distinction, we can stop being parents and end up being servants. Of course, your children retain their civil rights and every other human right granted in our society. At the same time, there should be no culture of entitlement in your home.

The important message is that, from here on out, the help that you provide your children is contingent upon their meeting your expectations. Turning everything into a privilege also makes it possible to reward children with things they probably take for granted (computer access, cell phones, new shoes, and the like).

As your child transitions to young adulthood, your relationship with him will become more transactional. That means your help is no longer a prerequisite and is provided as long as your expectations are met. Many children forget this. "I'm eighteen and I'm an adult!" they declare. The small print of that diatribe is that they want you to continue to pay for their lives or bail them out of trouble while leaving them alone. That isn't adulthood. Even when your child is an adult, there will be many areas where he will need your help. Make it clear, in an honest but supportive way, that the help comes with an exchange.

Cultivate a culture of reward. CEOs have to set limits from time to time, but they are not sheriffs. Leaders do more than enforce rules. If you are spending most of your time as a parent enforcing rules, then it will be harder to find the time to shape your family's culture.

It might sound like empty words, but perspective is important in your family culture. There is nothing to be gained by being punitive. Punishments are controversial deterrents and motivators. Even if you use punishment to get compliance, you still won't get kids to buy into the culture that you want.

Therefore, I would always advise that your family culture is one that looks to incentives as opposed to punishment. Instead of relying on punishment, set up family rules based on losing privileges when your expectations are not met. It's kind of like teaching a class where everyone starts off with an "A" and can maintain that grade if they complete all the assignments. With this approach, you avoid being the "bad guy." Everything rests on your child's sense of accountability and follow-through.

Like a skilled manager, you offer incentives for your kids to live up to your expectations and seek your approval. On the whole, this works much better than punishment. Through incentives, you can have a lasting influence on your child—one that continues during adolescence rather than wanes. The art of incentives starts with giving your child strategies to succeed.

To elicit the behaviors you want, model them. As a parent, your most important source of leadership is your own behavior. If you want your kids to express emotions appropriately, then show them the way. If you want your kids to keep their promises, then keep yours. If you want kids to regulate their emotions, then learn to regulate your own. Whatever you send out to your family will come back to you.

Your child may be struggling with accepting or communicating her feelings in therapy. Perhaps you could demonstrate how to do that when the opportunity arises. Maybe she is struggling with anger. Here is another opportunity for your leadership.

Effective modeling will do a lot to create the family culture that you want. This might even mean cutting off your drinking, even if you just drink socially. You don't want any fodder for your child to regress and use a hypocrisy argument against you.

The two main cards that your kids can play against you are hypocrisy and contradiction. Preventing hypocrisy really does boil down to something as simple and clichéd as "practicing what you preach." Your child will not be impressed by "do as I say and not as I do." No one is a saint. But if you love your child and you are not an alcoholic *and* you have liquor in the house, then it should be no problem for you to remove it. (If you struggle with doing this, then ask yourself what this fact reveals about you.)

Bottom line: *Function as a leader by focusing on key outcomes, revealing information on a need-to-know basis, distinguishing rights from privileges, making the rules, offering appropriate incentives, and modeling appropriate behavior. Ask yourself these questions:*

- What behaviors might signal that you are trying to micromanage your child? Could you change some of these behaviors?
- What are some examples of information or emotional content that you're processing right now that may not be wise to share with your child?
- Can you give some examples of the differences between rights and privileges based on recent events in your family?
- Have you made any promises to a child who's in treatment for addiction? If so, which of those promises are you realistically able to fulfill?
- In your personal approach to parenting, what is the balance between imposing punishments and offering incentives?
- Are there any significant discrepancies between your expectations for your kids and your own behavior? If so, how can you bring your words and actions into alignment?

Chapter 13

Don't Rewrite the Constitution—Setting Clear Expectations

As we have discussed thus far, consistency is an absolute necessity in parenting. When it comes to addiction, parents have to be there for the long run. Whenever we lose our cool, we lose our objectivity. Decisions become harder to make and far more personal.

Let's say you yell at your child Emily during an argument. She pushed your buttons on purpose. You feel bad about it, and a day later when she pushes your limits again, a part of you wants to yell louder. Another part of you wants to make up for yelling before. When you are trying to set your limits, how much do you give in? If you apologize for the day before, are you giving ground? Are you really being objective? Are you sure you aren't motivated by guilt? Is that a good way to make a decision? What kind of message are you sending if you apologize or don't? Will she hold this incident over your head if you give in?

Parents are baited by their children into power struggles like this all the time. Sometimes emotions run so high that it's hard to know what to do next.

This is where expectations come into play. There have to be parameters and rules in every relationship so that things stay objective. Without clear expectations, parents can do the right thing for a time, but eventually they get worn down by a child in distress. Children may work between one parent and another to get what they want. They will threaten. They will try to stir up guilt and anger.

So the first step in parenting through leadership is to set clear expectations. Expectations are basically a set of rules for the home. These rules are based on the family's values. The expectations are designed to save you from unnecessary emotional expenditure. And maintaining your emotional reserve will ensure that you are in this for the long haul. It will also ensure consistency.

Expectations should be communicated clearly. You should also allow for feedback and input from your children. Their suggestions are important, but since it is already established that your home is not a democracy, the final expectations are up to you. Once the expectations are set, make them work for you. They should be clear enough and simple enough to interpret. I often hear parents complain that their children misinterpret their intentions to help. Expectations allow you to step away from being the villain in your addicted child's story because you let the expectations govern. The interactions can be just as supportive, but they are less personal. A few other tips follow.

As I said earlier, when children are younger, it's natural to micromanage. We drive them around, talk to their teachers, and look over their shoulders even as we encourage independence. As they mature through adolescence, it's important that parents change their approach to a macromanagement style. This means that help from you now comes with expectations and contingencies. It also means that you make your expectations specific, but with the bigger picture in mind. Don't get lost in details.

You don't have to write a version of the Ten Commandments or the U.S. Constitution. Keep your expectations simple and basic. For example, expectations for a child in treatment might include the following:

- Respect everyone in the house.
- Attend all treatment activities.
- Complete expected chores.
- Engage in healthy relationships, which includes staying away from drug-using friends.

When family rules get much more complicated than that, they're subject to a variety of interpretations. And that's when a household can start to break down. As they often say in Alcoholics Anonymous, "Keep it simple."

Also, mind your emotional budget. Prioritize the expectations that have the biggest impact. For example, being compliant with treatment for substance abuse is a greater priority than making sure your child brushes his teeth nightly. (For more on this point, see chapter 7: "One Dollar a Day—Your Emotional Budget.")

Remember that effective rules apply to every child in the household. You don't want one of your kids to feel that she is the black sheep in the family. This doesn't mean that your non-drug-using children have the exact same rules. It does mean that the general paradigm of leadership, consistency, and governing with expectations goes for everyone in the home. It won't be hard to come up with fair expectations for the rest of the children in the house, regardless of age. Basically, if they are dependent on you or live under your roof, there need to be some expectations.

Finally, I advise parents to set aside two or three regular times each week for family discussions. During those times, you have tea, go for a walk, or eat dinner together. The meetings are preplanned. During the meetings, you can give your child effective praise for meeting expectations. Reminders of expectations, your child's performance for the week, and future considerations are all fair game during these meetings. You should also provide a forum for your child to discuss his perspectives, whether you feel they are reasonable or not. "Mom, I've been sober for a month now; can I go out next Friday?"

Outside of these regularly scheduled meetings, you don't have to get on your child's case very much. He will appreciate the lack of perceived "nagging." There will be fewer power struggles, and you will have the opportunity to macromanage in the way you want.

Bottom line: *Present your expectations as a short list of "do's" and "don'ts." Ask yourself these questions:*

- Can you express your current expectations of your children as a short list of clear and powerful statements? To answer this question, see if you can put your list in writing.
- Has your spouse or partner agreed to this list of expectations?
- Have you clearly communicated these expectations to your children? If not, when and how will you do so?

Chapter 14

Exit the Boxing Ring—the Top Signs of Power Struggles and How to Avoid Them

Power struggles drain a parent's emotional resolve. It matters not whether the parent is in the right or whether the parent is persuasive enough or powerful enough to win the conflict. In the end, all power struggles lead to negative outcomes. Like some of the other terms I've used in the book, power struggles are best defined pragmatically.

As such, you know that conversation with a child has degenerated into a power struggle when

- You're giving a top ten list of reasons to do something.
- You feel like an attorney who's arguing a case before a judge.
- Someone storms out of the room before the discussion (argument) is over.
- Your muscles get tense, and you notice that you're holding your breath.
- You feel like you've stepped into a boxing ring.
- There is tension in your interactions.

When you get deep into a power struggle, it's hard to step out of the ring and still emerge as a leader. When parents and kids try to communicate about emotionally laden issues at such a time, what usually happens is that tempers fly, parents get worn down, and kids believe they're getting nagged.

Teenagers sometimes like to have their parents step in the ring and duke it out verbally. But you can't win at that game. You're not perfect, and eventually you'll display a flaw in your emotional objectivity or leadership. Whatever you do, do not engage in power struggles. Even if you win the proverbial battle, you could lose the war.

That's easier said than done, right? Does this suggest we should just let our kids do whatever they want? Or, do we keep quiet and admonish them silently? I advise you to use an effective tool that I call the *broken record statement*. I learned the term and technique in my family therapy training from Susan Hazlett, Ph.D., at Duke University.

Have you ever called one of those automated customer-service hotlines? It could be an insurance company or an airline. They ask you to push one for English and two for Spanish and so on. The point of these annoying hotlines is to deter you from calling. They know it and you know it. It's hard to get mad at them because the computer-generated voice is oh-so-congenial, but it is what it is. Automated hotlines are designed to discourage calls.

If you ever find yourself in a power struggle with your teenager, don't engage. Instead, use the psychological underpinnings of the automated hotline—colored with some genuine compassion.

Broken record statements are designed to avoid power struggles. They deter kids from escalating conflicts in a personal direction. They allow parents to explain their positions without going into depth. They use repetition and the lack of engagement to dissuade arguments.

Broken record statements have three basic elements:

1. Restate a fair expectation of your child.

2. Validate your child without giving ground on the expectation.
3. Redirect the child to continue meeting your expectation, indicating clearly and tactfully that the discussion is over.

Here's an example: Let's assume that Billy is in residential treatment and has a complaint (there's not enough mustard in the cafeteria; his roommate snores; he didn't get his ADHD medicine; his counselor is mean). Some element of the complaint may be valid, but you sense that he is trying to use this to sabotage his care. He voices his complaints to you and delivers his logical arguments, hoping for your advocacy, or for a big intellectual debate that leads to this conclusion: "Mom and Dad, I don't think I belong here."

Using the broken record statement technique, you can respond with a statement such as this:

Our expectation is that you follow through with treatment (1). We know this can be hard, and we think you're doing a great job so far (2). Now, keep up the good work (3).

During a power struggle, your child will be ready with a comeback: "Wow, you are totally not listening to me."

In response, just go back to your original statement:

We know this can be hard, and we think you're doing a great job so far. You know our expectations. Now, keep up the good work.

"But wait," your child says. "The point I'm trying to make is. . . ."

Your response:

We know this can be hard, and we think you're doing a great job so far. Our expectation is that you follow through with treatment. Now, keep up the good work.

We don't call them "broken record statements" for nothing!

At first, kids are likely to protest: "You're not listening to me! You're just saying the same thing over and over again. You sound like a robot. Are you crazy?"

If things continue to escalate, you might have to leave the area or hang up the phone with words such as: *When you are calmer, we can talk.*

Eventually, though, on a deeper psychological level, your child will come to understand. And he will stop engaging you on that level.

Broken record statements can be especially effective when you allow separate times for free-flowing, unstructured discussions with your child. Broken record statements sound simple, but using them effectively takes a lot of practice. It's worth it. This strategy allows parents to defuse the hot issues and set them aside for another time when cooler heads prevail and conflicts can actually be resolved. Over time, you will shape your child's behaviors and interactions with you without losing emotional reserve.

Bottom line: *Recognize the signs of a power struggle and defuse it with a broken record statement: restate, validate, and redirect. Ask yourself these questions:*

- What are some examples of power struggles that you've experienced with your child in the past?
- What power struggles might surface in the future?
- What's an example of a broken record statement that you could use with your child? Try rehearsing this with someone you know.

Chapter 15

Present Your Child with a United Front

Imagine that you are in a hospital and quite sick with an unknown illness. A team of physicians, me included, comes by your bed on morning rounds. You are scared. Your family is scared. And frankly, the team is at a loss for immediate answers.

Physicians understand that, in moments like this, our facial expressions, our body language, and even our tone of voice matter. Everyone loses morale if we lose our objectivity. If we argue in front of you about treatment options, or if our faces communicate a sense of fear to you, how much confidence will you really have in us?

Zero. None. *Nada*.

In a situation like this, it doesn't matter if we are the best medical team in the world. We won't instill confidence in our skill because we haven't demonstrated our leadership.

In the same way, parents who openly disagree with each other in front of their kids about how to handle a family issue are not demonstrating confidence, let alone emotional objectivity or leadership.

Following are the key points to keep in mind.

First, present a united front to your children when it comes to the most important family expectations. Don't let them go to Dad for one set of requests and to Mom for another.

In some families, for example, one parent routinely fields questions about getting an extra allowance, and the other parent gets all the last-minute pleas to stay overnight at a friend's house. This is a perfect setup for parental contradiction. It almost guarantees that one parent will be in the dark about a key issue at any given time. Make it clear that important or controversial requests need to be approved by all parent figures.

Second, don't argue in front of your children. In times of crisis, you and your partner need to be the same person to your children. Your confidence and unity demonstrate leadership. If you disagree with each other or have not yet established a united opinion on a certain matter and need to have a discussion, then do that behind closed doors—away from your children. If one of you says something spontaneously, without consent from the other person, go with it for the time being unless the comment is way out of line. Then, come to an agreement later in a private conversation and make necessary adjustments. Remember, parents do get to change the rules.

Third, avoid nonverbal communication that signals contradiction. Some mothers and fathers indulge in "secret" signals of disagreement during a family discussion. Mom elbows Dad after he makes a comment, or Dad rolls his eyes when Mom starts crying. Parents tend to lack awareness of such nonverbal communication or assume that kids just don't notice it. In reality, the signals are obvious to everyone.

In the face of a key revelation about your child—such as incidence of drug use—act like you already know what happened. Maybe you actually *don't* know all the details about how much your child used or with whom. But if you knew that your child was experimenting, that's enough. You don't have to pretend that you're omniscient. But on the other hand, there's no need to act like you're clueless. You can often elicit more details by asking your child to volunteer them ("I'd like to hear what *you* have to say about how this happened"). In a similar way, always act like you have a plan for responding to the issue, even if the details are still fuzzy in your mind ("Your mom and I have been talking about what to do about this, and we'll let you know very soon"). The key principle is to avoid situations where you're taken by surprise, shocked, and confused about how to respond. The result of this is that your child dictates the pace, tone, and content of the conversation, meaning that your leadership is lost.

The same rules apply when your child is in treatment. Always act like you are a step ahead of your child. You can be surprised and disappointed to some degree, but make sure you present it as one of the possible contingencies that you expected. Now, feel free to hound and interrogate the clinicians treating your child if the opportunity arises. Ask all the questions you want and receive guidance. But when you talk to your child, you must communicate confidence.

Bottom line: *Exercise leadership by presenting kids with messages that are free of internal contradictions and interpersonal conflicts. Ask yourself these questions:*

- If someone recorded a video of you talking to your child at a crucial moment, would that recording reveal someone whose verbal and nonverbal communication sent the same basic message?
- When it comes to basic expectations for your child, are you and your spouse or partner on the same page? Do you intentionally or inadvertently throw each other under the bus? What could you do differently to be on the same team?

Chapter 16

The Danger of Bleeding Emotions

We have established that as leaders in your home, you have to carry yourself with a certain conviction. Your leadership has to be reflected in all aspects of your person: your body language, your tone of voice, and your facial expressions. But how and when do we show our kids our feelings? When is it okay and when is it inappropriate? Now that we have discussed some basics of parenting through leadership, it's time to be more specific on this matter.

When a child struggles with the grips of addiction, emotions carry the day. Our intuitions betray us. Trust is shattered. Blame is cast. Bitterness and resentments seed irrepressibly. Families once founded on cohesiveness become divisive. The very instincts that parents have relied on over the years to nurture and support their offspring are turned against them by lies and manipulation.

Most rational and disciplined parents rally in moments of crisis. They turn to tried-and-true parenting traditions. They go out of their way to communicate their love and concern in the most sincere ways. Mothers advocate blindly to protect their children from harm. Fathers lecture in vain with pleas for logic and sound judgment.

At times, there appear to be genuine breakthroughs. Desperation demands a yearning for hope, however unsettling. Compromises are made, enabling ensues, and a tentative truce is cast.

This is an uneasy and temporary peace, and it's created while emotions are bleeding in all directions.

Often, addiction surfaces again. Parents and loved ones bear down and persevere. They enter this vicious cycle over and over again, but their resolve is slowly eroded and scarred by the disease. In the end, their hope is supplanted by the lingering sting of betrayed confidence. Everyone feels emotionally exhausted.

How, then, do we parent during times of family crisis when our best-laid intentions seem to yield so little? You can start by remembering to show your emotions to your children only when these two conditions are met:

- when your emotions are positive
- when your children meet your expectations

Otherwise, you may lose your emotional objectivity and your leadership—something that children can immediately sense and try to use to their advantage.

This is an area where I see a lot of parents *saying* the right things, but not *doing* the right things. Nonverbal cues of bleeding emotions—such as a trembling voice or a tear trailing down your cheek—can undermine your leadership, even when you say all the "right" things to your children. If you were to shoot a movie of a scene where parents are bleeding emotions in the face of a defiant child, you'd see that the child is in control, no matter what the parents are saying. To prevent this outcome, avoid being too transparent emotionally. To put it another way, an addicted child can be like a shark in water. When you bleed emotions, they can go in for an attack.

Please understand that I am not telling you to repress your emotions or to express only the emotions that are politically correct. I am not asking you to be a stoic. You can share your unvarnished feelings with lots of people. Share them with your spouse or partner. Share them behind closed doors with staff members at your child's treatment center. In contexts like these, you can bleed emotions at will. You can shake, cry, scream, shout—whatever it takes to discharge your feelings and regain perspective. Just don't do this disproportionately in front of your child.

It is just as important to work on showering your child with affection when she meets expectations. Traditionally, doctors are notorious for pointing out the flaws in others. It's our job. My job many times is to highlight the 5 percent of a client's life that needs improvement, not the 95 percent that might be going well. Parents are good at noticing when things go off the rail as well. We are not so great at sufficiently praising our children for doing the right things or meeting small expectations. Things like that can be taken for granted. But doing so causes us to miss a great opportunity to shape our children's behaviors.

Parents are frequently surprised to find out that they really aren't very good at praising their children when they meet expectations. Some find that it comes off as cheesy or insincere. But even false compliments work. For example, a stereotypical used-car salesman may ingratiate himself to his customers by showering them with false compliments. But he still moves cars. So even if your child finds your new tendency to praise achievement suspect, it will influence him with repetition.

Let's say that one expectation for your child in treatment was for him to become committed to sobriety.

"Dad, I think it's time that I started to make some changes," he says. "So I went to three group meetings this week."

Taking time to compose yourself, you pause and turn around, making full eye contact with your child with a genuine smile. "I'm proud that you are committed to being healthier."

One important caveat to remember is that you do not want to heap praise for halfhearted efforts or empty promises. Parents who begrudgingly praise children when expectations are not fully met are usually walking on eggshells with a volatile child. It's a sign that they are not in control. You should encourage progress, of course, but you don't want your child to feel like you are satisfied with half measures.

Next, you want to set up scenarios around the home where the chances that your child will meet smaller expectations are high. For example, he could help you cook or aid in a household project. Though these aren't the explicit expectations you have made clear with your child, they are keeping in the spirit of them. Whenever you see behavior that you like, praise it. Go overboard. Slobber all over him. Over time, he will start to seek your approval once again.

Bottom line: *Engage with your child only when you can be calm and positive. Ask yourself these questions:*

- Do you ever say the right thing but communicate the wrong message via body language or facial expressions?
- Do you react (with body language, facial expression, tone of voice, and so on) when your child emotes in an unwanted way? Do these reactions undermine your leadership role?
- Do you take time to notice when your child is behaving in the way you want? How do you praise your child for it?

Chapter 17

Investing for the Long Term—Preparing for the Ups and Downs of Recovery

When our child is addicted, we want to do everything possible. We'd sacrifice just about anything. But we must remember two things.

First, *addiction is a chronic disease.* As such, your involvement in it will resemble a marathon and not a sprint. While it's great if your child shows progress in recovery after the first attempt at treatment, you want to make sure you have something left in the tank just in case.

Second, *leadership depends on foresight.* It's important that you sit down with other family members and consider your limitations. For every decision you make on behalf of your child, and every limit you set to hold your ground, ask yourself if you are ready for the possible outcomes, both good and bad. Think through the potential consequences.

Let's go through a couple of scenarios.

Imagine that a treatment center is available for your child. Like many others, it's not cheap. In fact, it's the most expensive program on your list. You've done your research, however, and you believe this is the best option for you and your family.

What happens if this treatment doesn't work out? Let's assume that your child isn't cooperative and does not benefit from treatment. How will this affect your decision making the next time she is in need?

Will you resent your child for not making the most of her opportunity? Will you extend yourself financially to the point where such resentments are inevitable? Do you feel you would resent your child for anything short of absolute success in treatment? If the answer to these questions is yes, then you're likely to feel incredible disappointment if the outcome of the expensive treatment isn't what you wanted it to be. And this will, in turn, undermine your emotional objectivity for future decisions.

Now for a different scenario.

This time, imagine that your child has had some success with treatment and has been sober for a few months. Trust starts to build again. Everything appears to be going well. You discover on one unfortunate day, however, that your child has relapsed. What are your responsibilities at this point? How do you approach her? How will you express your emotions in an appropriate way?

Treatment decisions should be made while considering the risks and rewards. I would advise processing the pros and cons of different treatment programs with someone who can support you, such as a therapist who's referred kids to those programs before. And as soon as your child enters treatment, prepare yourself for the possibility of relapse. How will you handle it—not just the use, but also the deception?

Hopefully, relapse will never happen. But even in cases where your child stays sober throughout treatment and afterward, there will be ups and downs.

Here is some imagery that can help. People in treatment often improve over time. Yet their progress resembles the stock market. Over the long term, the market will go up, but there will be many jagged ups and downs along the way. If you have a short-term perspective, then you'll believe that the stocks that are going up will *continue* to go up forever. Stocks that are going down will seem apocalyptic. Long-term investors generally do better than short-term investors because they stay far more objective. This metaphor applies well to thinking through the ups and downs of recovery. The key is not to get too excited when your child is doing well, and not to get personally discouraged when your child struggles.

At Hazelden, I often see parents who are deeply and emotionally involved in their child's treatment. Most of the time, this is a touching and beautiful gesture. But sometimes I wonder if the parents are working harder than their child is. Some of these parents jump with every high point in treatment and crash with every low. They hang on every turn and analyze every call. I wonder if they're so vigilant about details and updates that they'll run themselves into the ground.

I truly can't blame parents for acting this way. In similar circumstances, I might do the same. At the same time, I wonder how they are possibly going to last over the long haul if they continue their involvement at such a frenetic pace. Will they get exhausted? What will happen if they are faced with another downturn and have little left to give? Will they resent their child and situation, and then refuel their commitment with unhealthy doses of guilt and feelings of failure? Bitterness is a by-product of such endeavors.

Bottom line: *Remember not to get too excited when your child does well in early sobriety—and not to get overly discouraged during times of struggle or relapse. Ask yourself these questions:*

- As a parent, do you consistently feel overextended?
- How are you going to manage emotional reserves, your finances, and your involvement in your child's recovery for the long term?

Chapter 18

More on Boundaries: The Under-Invested and Over-Invested Parent

I'm going to build on the previous chapter by discussing two extremes of parent involvement in a child's recovery from addiction.

First is the *under-invested parent*. These parents are prone to denial. They are likely to say things such as this:

- My family is just fine.
- I can't see any real issues with the kids.
- If my child truly is addicted, then it's his problem, not mine; there's not much I can do about it.

Under-invested parents often care a great deal about their child. They are frequently good providers and sufficient role models in better times. However, the emotional toll of dealing with their child's addiction is just too much. In the end, these parents believe their child's addiction might be a kind of indictment on them and their parenting style. This can drive parents to push their child away inadvertently or cause them to see their child's addiction as a by-product of something they are completely removed from. Under-invested parents are sometimes called out by their child for not being more involved. This can start a vicious cycle where a parent might blame the child, or scold him for raising false accusations. Under-invested parents may collude with the child to blame a third party (such as an estranged spouse) for the child's problems, which serves the same function as leaving themselves out of their child's addiction completely.

It is important to remember the deck of cards analogy. Most parents are not responsible for their child's addiction. Most parents are also far from perfect. So there is a place in between where parents can admit that they could have done a few things better as parents while not shouldering the blame for the addiction. Instead of wasting your energy minimizing your culpability as a part of the problem, realize that you are a major part of the solution moving forward. So take a deep breath. You can say you need to improve as a parent in the context of your child's addiction while not feeling culpable.

The *over-invested parent*—often well-meaning—goes to the opposite extreme of being too involved in the child's treatment process. There are many different kinds of over-invested parents. These parents simply cannot handle any failure or distress in their child. They may have a long history of over-investing in visits to therapists or physicians but do not fully trust them. They don't know when to advocate for their child and when to let their child advocate for herself.

I have seen well-intentioned over-invested parents in multiple settings. The classic example is with school refusal, which is when a child (usually in grade school) is anxious and will not go to school. The child may make frequent visits to the nurse's station, or blame the teachers as being mean, or complain about a number of physical ailments. The standard of care is first to have the child go to school, and then do any workups for possible medical issues on the side, as to not reinforce the school refusal.

Some parents struggle with a situation like this. They find themselves fighting a battle on two fronts. On the one hand, they suspect their child is anxious and needs to go to school to overcome the anxiety. On the other, they can't help but investigate their child's complaints in a not-so-subtle way. The parents then interrogate school officials and make doctor's appointments. Conflicts and suspicions arise on the parents' part about the very people who are there to care for their child. There are times when such explorations are fruitful, but the point is that the child recognizes this behavior in the parents and misinterprets it as reinforcement for not changing. The parents can then become even more critical of the school system and health care professionals. In the end, the child will never go back to school as long as the parents continue this battle.

Similar situations arise in addiction treatment. Kids will tell their parents that they are motivated to get well, but they are hindered by something in the treatment itself. They blame everything from the food to the quality of staff to the treatment philosophy. The question is not whether their complaints have legitimacy, but in how the parents choose to handle those complaints. They can focus on the big picture and ask a few questions behind the scenes, or their kids can wind them up and send them on one hopeless crusade after another. It isn't until the child has failed multiple treatments that the parents finally realize that the problem wasn't where they thought it was.

Sometimes over-invested parents are described as *hypervigilant*. Hypervigilance implies an intense alertness or overreaction disproportionate to the requirements of the situation. Over-invested parents struggle with emotional objectivity. Give them feedback about this point, and they'll find it hard to take. They can easily wind up mad at their child, mad at treatment professionals, and mad at the world in general. Eventually, they feel guilty about their level of anger and attempt to compensate by loosening up on their boundaries. This sets up a negative feedback loop: The smallest setback triggers the parents into emotional extremes, and their kids react in kind. When these parents come to visit the treatment center, the kids may actually regress—that is, they seem to lose the gains they made over previous days or weeks.

It can be strange to see your relationship with your child through this filter of emotional boundaries. It might seem to you that the relationship is more transactional than loving. The point, however, is that we all have limits. If we cannot stay within our boundaries, we cannot consistently "be there" for our children.

Sometimes I have to remind parents not to work harder in treatment than their kids. Parents have to remember what they can control and what they cannot. This division of labor is critical. Substance abuse professionals can help with this. Talk to them early and often about how you should and shouldn't help out.

At the end of the day, your child's recovery is on her. Clinicians, parents, and supportive friends can provide the tools and encouragement. But in the end, she must make the decision to go through the door of recovery.

This brings me to a couple of my favorite metaphors.

You are like a house on the street, with a picket fence and a lawn. Your children, partner or spouse, and other family members have houses next to yours or across the street, all with their own respective lawns and fences. You can hang out at their houses, spend time with them on their lawns, and attend barbecues in their backyards. But if you want to experience peace of mind, never forget where your property ends and their property begins.

Let's try one more metaphor. I used to love *The Giving Tree* by Shel Silverstein, and it's still one of my favorite books. It's about a boy and a tree. The tree gives the boy all of its bounty and resources as he ages. In the end, the tree has nothing to give but a resting place for the boy, who is now an elderly man. The story is a great metaphor for parenting.

Like trees that continually bear fruit, the best gifts always keep giving. A parent's love fills a child's tree with fruit and bounty. Because that love is unconditional, fruits that are plucked grow anew with time. The thing to remember is that every tree has a different rate for replenishing its goods. If fruit is harvested faster than the tree can replenish, then the tree eventually is damaged. The tree's willingness to offer bounty does not waver, but its capacity for giving does. For the tree to produce fruit for the long run, you have to sustain that tree.

In a similar way, I have met too many parents who give until nothing is left. These parents become exhausted. They are scarred repeatedly by guilt and bitterness. Sustenance can come in the form of therapy for the parent, which I highly recommend.

Support from family and other parents who have gone through the same situation is also part of the healing process. I know that many of us value our privacy, and the thought of going to meetings like Al-Anon may make us feel awkward. But think of it as a way to recharge your own batteries, and you just might see it differently.

Bottom line: *You can't save children from drowning if you deny that they are in trouble—or if you are too busy treading water yourself. Ask yourself these questions:*

- Do you ever minimize your role in your child's addiction for fear of what that might mean?
- Do you find yourself fighting a battle on two fronts when your child is in addiction treatment? That is, are you skeptical of both your child and the people who treat him? What could you do differently?
- Are you pacing your support for your child in crisis so that you can sustain your help for the long run?

Chapter 19

Do I Kick My Kid Out of the House? Your Values Are Your Bottom Line

One of the first things I ask parents of kids in treatment is: How far are you willing to go? What will you allow, and what won't you allow? When it comes to your child's behavior, what's your bottom line? As a physician, I can't tell you what your bottom line is. I can't dictate your values to you. That's for you to choose. The tough fact is that every choice has consequences.

If your child repeatedly violates your expectations, you might decide that there will come a time to send an ultimatum, like kicking him out of the house. This choice has consequences that might include your child's ending up on the street, or experiencing legal consequences, like sitting in jail overnight when you don't bail him out.

On the other hand, you might decide that your fundamental value is safety. If you kick your child out of the house, she could overdose. She might get raped. She might get hepatitis. These are the realities of addiction. And your bottom line may be that you can't let anything like this happen under any circumstances. You might have to weigh the risk of your child's overdosing on the street versus on your watch. More important, you will have to determine which will sting more. Most parents decide that, in the end, if there is a risk of harm either way, they would rather feel like they did what they could to stop the addiction, as opposed to indirectly condoning a downhill slide by turning away or ignoring.

There are no easy solutions here. Parents really have to exercise leadership. They need to sit down, call everyone to the table, grapple with the issues, and talk about how family values translate into day-to-day choices, including the really gut-wrenching decisions. Parents must also examine local laws that pertain to parental responsibility. If your child is a minor, you have certain legal responsibilities to provide a home and certain levels of care. But you may still have legal options available, and when that magical eighteenth birthday arrives, your options expand even more.

The frameworks for parenting that I offer in this book are flexible enough to accommodate a variety of values. Ask your physician, therapist, and other professionals to sit down with you and help you sort through the pros and cons of any potential choice.

Please make time for this conversation. It's not easy. But it is necessary.

Ultimately, though, none of us can tell you what choice to make. I can only tell you that if you *don't* make a choice, then you can end up hanging on to the status quo. You can end up enabling your child's drug use and eventual breakdown. You can end up as part of the problem rather than the solution. Your family boundaries need to be clearly understood by everyone involved and then adhered to. If those boundaries begin to waver or grow soft, then you'll lose your leadership edge. I hope that you will avoid having to make such difficult decisions; however, much of the parenting advice in this book won't have any bite if you lack the conviction to follow through in these moments of crisis.

Bottom line: *Based on your ultimate values, choose what you'll do if your child develops a pattern of relapsing. Ask yourself these questions:*

- How much time and money are you willing and able to invest in treatment?
- How do you want to respond if your child is consistently relapsing a year from today? Two years from today? Five years?
- Are you and your spouse or partner on the same page as to what your bottom lines are? Do you believe you will follow through on your convictions if need be?

Chapter 20

Extinction Burst and the Case for Consistency

You and I are trapped in a room. Let's say we are locked in but don't know it yet. I try turning the doorknob, and the door doesn't budge. At this point, we don't throw up our hands and say, "Well, we tried. Looks like we're locked in." No. On the contrary, we try opening the door ten different ways. We knock on the door to see if anyone will let us out. We might use a credit card or an office tool to jimmy the door open. As our efforts fail, we become increasingly frustrated. Our efforts then take a more desperate and serious turn. Finally, when we have exhausted all of our options for escape, we accept our fate temporarily. We accept that we are locked in.

Unwanted behaviors do not fade slowly and consistently, not for us and not for our children. If a certain behavior gets us a certain result on a few occasions, then we will expect said result from then on. When that result is no longer produced, we don't just stop that behavior. We might temporarily increase that behavior until we are convinced of its futility. Though not a strict academic definition, this is what is called an extinction burst. Before an unwanted behavior goes away, it paradoxically crescendos, then subsides.

People who are addicted are used to a certain status quo in their disease. They do not want to surrender it. When parents become wiser and try to set limits, the child will increase willful behaviors to sustain the status quo. The only way to combat this is to be consistent. Over time, the child's behaviors will extinguish, and he will recalibrate to the new norm in your house.

I have parents who come into my office and tell me all the things they have tried to set the right limits and boundaries at home: "I've called the police and even threw him out of the house." What they didn't do was remain consistent. Since they weren't consistent with their limit-setting methods, their child's undesirable behavior did not extinguish. That made the parents employ over-the-top tactics, not knowing that consistency was more important than severity of action.

On a related issue, some parents try to set limits (such as a curfew) and the child will escalate the conflict quickly, hoping to get the parents into an appeasement or compromising state of mind: "Well, this certainly isn't working; maybe we need to be softer or try a different approach." If you are being emotionally objective and are operating as a leader to foster the right culture in your home, then my advice would actually be to continue on your path. Chances are, if you are doing the right thing, you will be met with resistance from your child on some level initially.

As I've stated before, consistency requires a culture of emotional objectivity and leadership. If you are firing on all cylinders, don't get discouraged because of a lack of early returns. Stick to the principles. The only caveat is when your child raises the ante by threatening harm to herself or others. In this situation, calmly call the police or 911. Don't take chances with her safety. Take every suicidal threat and gesture seriously by covering your bases and getting medical attention, but do so without letting your child know that you are compromised in any way. Don't give up hope. Sometimes, it really is darkest before dawn.

Bottom line: *If you are cultivating the right culture in your home consistently, do not give up hope when your child's behaviors escalate. Ask yourself these questions:*

- Have you tried to set limits on your child only to have him get rageful? What do you think he was really trying to accomplish with that gesture? How did you respond? Did you change your stance?
- Do you have a team of people and professionals who can support your efforts to be consistent through encouragement and objective feedback? If not, how could you get one?
- Have you ever experienced extinction burst yourself? Did anyone ever try to extinguish a bad habit or behavior in you, only to have you increase the frequency or intensity of that behavior before giving it up?

Chapter 21

Comparisons Are Odious; or, It's Okay That Your Family Is Different

During my time in medical school, I took a break to travel overseas with friends. We spent some time in Amsterdam, a really interesting and beautiful city. One day we went to a Burger King there for lunch. I ordered a burger and a Diet Coke. After drinking up all the soda, I went back up to the counter for a refill.

"We don't give free refills," the guy at the counter said.

"What are you talking about?" I said. "This is a Burger King. I'm from the United States, and all the Burger Kings there give free refills."

"Not in Amsterdam," the guy said. "It's different here. If we gave free refills, we would be out of Coke within a few hours after we open."

Now, I'm not sure if this is just what that guy at Burger King believed or if it is a true cultural phenomenon. The point I want to emphasize here isn't about burgers or refills. The point is that we often forget how culture influences policy.

Politicians often make this mistake. They take some broad, sweeping social policy from another country without understanding that country's cultural and economic idiosyncrasies, then assume it will work just as well here on the merits of the idea alone. People do the same thing with recommending diets to each other, assuming everyone will have the same degree of success. Addicted youth share information the same way. "Hey, Mom, this is how Fred manages to use without getting in trouble, and he still gets good grades. I think I could do that."

Sometimes kids attempt to justify their drug-using behavior by making comparisons with other families and even other cultures:

- "My friend Bill gets to drink a glass of wine at Thanksgiving dinner."
- "In Europe, the legal drinking age is sixteen."
- "At school, this exchange student from Amsterdam says that they sell marijuana in the coffee shops over there."

Comments like that remind me of a line from Shakespeare: "Comparisons are odious."

Beware the family comparison, the culture comparison, and all the rest. When it comes to leading your family, none of those comparisons matter. The only thing that matters is doing what's right for your child. As we discussed, cultures and situations in families differ. A notion that works for one may not work for another. Children will prefer a smorgasbord of rules in the home, however, picked carefully from one family, then another, to ensure that they get what they want in the end. Be one step ahead of them.

This is especially true if your child has risk factors for addiction or other mental health issues due to family history. It's important for each family to assess their own risks for addiction and act accordingly, just as they would do for risks of diabetes or heart disease. If six of your relatives were alcoholics, then it's pointless to compare your policies on drug use to the policies of a family with no history of addiction. It's okay for you to ban your child from having wine at Thanksgiving, no matter what Bill's family does.

In Western psychology, whether we like it or not, Freudian influences are powerful. As a result, parents get bombarded by a hidden but powerful message: *If your child gets addicted, it's your fault. You did something wrong when your child was an infant, and you're living with the results right now.* In response, parents feel terrible and scour themselves for flaws. They try to pinpoint the time and place when they screwed up with their child. This is the dynamic that launches parents into needless comparisons with other families.

Remember, every family is different. Children grow and mature at different rates, families have varied genetic histories, and parents hold different values about drugs and alcohol. By making comparisons with and measuring against other families, parents undermine their emotional objectivity and leadership. Remember that no one is perfect, and whether or not you believe you made mistakes in the past, put the past on the back burner. All that matters, really, is the family culture you develop and what you do for your child today.

Bottom line: *Your family represents a unique culture, and it's okay to set limits with this in mind. Ask yourself these questions:*

- What is your family history of addiction and other chronic illnesses?
- Does your family history make a difference as you think about what kind of culture you want to create for your family? If so, how?
- How might your family culture differ from the family cultures of your child's peer group?

Chapter 22

Motivate Your Child with the Bullshit Scale

I was at an addiction conference once and heard a lecture from James Finch, M.D., from North Carolina, who gave a talk on motivational interviewing. The analogies and phrases he used were so moving that I started to adopt the spirit of some of them into my work with youth.

To paraphrase some of his ideas, I ask kids in treatment to honestly rate their motivation to stay sober on an increasing scale:

1. I *should* be sober.
2. I *need* to be sober.
3. I *want* to be sober.
4. I *will* be sober.

Dr. Finch compared this to getting married. On your wedding day, you don't say to your future spouse: I *should* marry you. Or I *want* to marry you. No, what you say is: I *will*. I *promise*. I *do*.

Notice that each of those statements gains strength as you go down the list. *Should* sounds like a moral imperative but could simply exist in our fantasies ("I should go to the gym"). *Need* increases the urgency, at least in our thoughts. With *want*, your tasks are starting to line up with your desires. And *will* is a firm commitment to act.

I now give kids what I call a "bullshit scale." There are times in life when you tell yourself something, and you just know in your heart if it is true or not. For example, when you tell someone you love her, you will know it as either true or false in your heart. In addiction, it may be something like *I know my use is now out of control.*

The basic premise is this: Listen to yourself when you make such a statement. You might think that you're being philosophical and profound. But if you really listen, you'll know whether it rings true or false. And if it's bullshit, you'll just know it in your bones.

Many kids enter treatment with some idea about wanting to be sober. But addiction is a tricky disease that hinders our ability to make honest appraisals. Some will believe that their commitment for sobriety is strong initially, only to find that their intent does not match their convictions. Others who are apprehensive about recovery find that they have more conviction than they thought.

Kids get this. What we do in treatment is get them to line their intentions up—to go from thinking of sobriety as just a good idea to making a firm commitment.

When I talk to young people in session, I just ask the question directly: "On a scale of one to ten, what's your motivation to get better?"

"Ten," they often say. "My motivation is really high."

"Okay," I respond. "Now I want to hear it on the bullshit scale. Tell me, can you say, 'I *should* be sober'?"

"Yes."

"Can you say, 'I *need* to be sober'?"

"Yes."

"Can you say, 'I *want* to be sober'?"

"Uh…yeah."

"Okay, now can you really say, 'I *will* be sober'?"

(Pause.) "Okay. Yeah. *Maybe I'm not quite there yet.*"

After this conversation goes on for a while, kids understand how to reconcile their intent to get better with their actual commitment for change.

Let's flip this scenario around for parents. As I have said before, parents find themselves on a parallel track with their children in recovery. Sometimes there are things in the home or in your parenting approach or in your relationships that need to change. And parents also need to make an honest appraisal of their commitment to that change.

The change required might be about a commitment to set firm boundaries or the commitment to let go of ineffective emotional expression. It might have to do with getting rid of alcohol in your home or confronting someone else in the family about their use. On a scale of one to ten, how would you rate your own commitment to change? Can you clearly articulate what *should* be taking place in your household and your child's recovery, and move up the scale to *will*?

Bottom line: *Your child's clinicians can use the bullshit scale to help your kid upgrade vague intentions to clear promises. More important, try it out with yourself. Think about something you need to change in your life for your child's recovery. Ask yourself these questions:*

- As you monitor your commitment for change as a parent, do you use the word *should*, *need*, *want*, or *will*?
- If you can only say *should*, what could help you say *need*? If you can say *need*, what would it take to get you to *want*? And finally, if you are at *want*, what could take you to *will*?

Frameworks for Understanding Mental Health

Chapter 23

Understanding Mental Health Issues in the Context of Addiction—Which Comes First?

I get more questions about mental health issues in addiction treatment than anything else, and by a long shot. It isn't just because of my profession. The interplay between mental health and addiction can be downright confusing for parents and clinicians alike. To borrow a phrase from Winston Churchill, trying to figure out the relationship between psychiatric and addiction problems can be "a riddle, wrapped in a mystery, inside an enigma."

There are other hidden forces at work for parents when looking at addiction and mental health problems. These forces can also bias clinicians, as I will point out later.

But first, let's look at a typical case I might be involved in.

Miguel is a teenager who is starting outpatient treatment for drug addiction. There is a strong family history of addiction on both sides. There was a divorce in the family when he was eight, and he reports feeling estranged from his father for a number of years thereafter. He has always been shy and has trouble making new friends on his own. He was bullied in elementary school because of his weight, compounding his social problems and self-image.

If that weren't enough, Miguel has struggled in school because of a learning disability. In the past, he has made it clear how shameful and different he felt for having to leave his "normal" classes to receive "special" instruction for two hours a day—not to mention that his two older siblings were honor students.

The few friends that Miguel has made have turned on him recently because of the addiction. He also feels traumatized by the loss of a close using friend who overdosed not long ago. Miguel is on an antidepressant and was recently diagnosed with ADHD in addition to his learning issues.

Miguel's mother recognized that he had a number of challenges growing up. She overcompensated by giving him too much latitude out of sympathy and concern. Perhaps some of this was spurred by her guilt about her divorce.

When Miguel started to use drugs, he appeared at first to be more social and outgoing. Seeing this as a positive thing, his mother didn't condone but didn't condemn his drug use, hoping that it would just be a rite of passage for a late-blooming young man who never got a fair shake.

When Miguel's use got out of control, she had a hard time putting the brakes on his use and getting him to comply with house rules, as these were big shifts in the family culture. He got used to manipulating, lying to, and bullying his mother. She finally had enough when he was suspended from school for drug possession, and she enrolled him in treatment. Since that time, she has been getting help herself and has been making earnest efforts to set the right expectations and limits at home.

Fast-forward in time: Now, Miguel has been in treatment for two weeks. He is sober, with strict supervision and drug testing by his parents, who are still divorced but united on this front. Everyone is aware that he has been depressed for the past few months. He has been having passive suicidal thoughts at times but says he would never actually hurt himself.

One day, Miguel comes home and is sullen. A casual request by his mother results in an angry outburst from him. He says he isn't an addict and accuses his mother of overreacting by sending him to treatment. He says he was just depressed for a long time and was looking for a way out with drugs. He adds that he has learned his lesson, so she might as well take him out of treatment, and that her "forceful" efforts to get him sober are making his depression worse. Finally, he says, the treatment team isn't doing "anything about my depression or trauma at all."

The facts of Miguel's using history suggest that he was more than a casual drug abuser. He pawned his favorite items and even sacrificed his relationship with his first and only girlfriend for drugs. On the other hand, his mother wonders if he is right. Maybe it was the depression all along. If he'd only grown up feeling better about himself, if he hadn't been bullied or estranged from his father for years, might that have prevented his use? Secretly, his mother also struggles with guilt for not taking him for help earlier. She regrets her inability to "protect" him in the past and wonders if she has made the wrong call.

The mother is torn about how to respond to Miguel's yelling and pleas. She thinks that he might be trying to manipulate once again, but she also wonders if he's telling the truth and taking her to task for being closed-minded. She wants to set limits but doesn't want to push too far, fearing it will push him away or make his depression worse. She doesn't know if his anger signals that he's using again. She wants to call the treatment team and ask them why his depression isn't being taken care of.

So many mixed sentiments with no clear solutions—what is a mother to do? This is the kind of situation that parents face all too often. When it comes to mental health issues and addiction, what came first? Which one is more important? How should we respond, and who is accountable for what?

Up to now, you've learned the basics of a parenting philosophy emphasizing culture, leadership, and emotional objectivity. These techniques will work best when applied within the context that I provide in this part of the book. You don't have to become a mental health expert to sail these waters. But you do need a solid framework to understand how mental health and addiction cross paths.

My goal is not to provide a comprehensive review of every mental health issue your child could ever have. However, there are a number of perspectives I would like to share with you—perspectives that will help you navigate through the confusing world of co-occurring addiction and mental health diagnoses.

The following chapters will help you see your child the way I do—not just as a list of diagnoses and not as a helpless victim in a tragic story line. Instead, my goal is for us to see kids as they really are—young souls who are both full of risk and full of promise.

The emphasis in the following pages is on *how* to look at the interplay of mental health and addiction—not *what* you know about them factually. There are many books on the details of mental health diagnoses and treatment. But trust me—the larger perspective that I offer in this part of the book is more important.

It boggles my mind that there isn't more out there for parents on these perspectives. After all, no one interprets all diagnoses the same way. Some may criticize my attempts to simplify the complicated world of addiction and mental health so directly. But as Einstein said, "Any intelligent fool can make things bigger, more complex, and more violent. It takes a touch of genius—and a lot of courage—to move in the opposite direction."

Well, there's no genius in this book. But if you are willing to be courageous with me, I will share with you what I hold to be true.

Bottom line: *If Miguel's story sounds even vaguely familiar to you, suspend your beliefs on mental health and addiction for a moment, and approach the following chapters with an open mind.*

Chapter 24

Basic Facts about the Developing Brain; or, Why Teens Can Have Good Logic and Poor Judgment

One of my favorite *Saturday Night Live* skits of all time made fun of stock footage in kung fu movies. Have you ever noticed in action-movie fight scenes that when a gang of villains attacks the hero, one fighter attacks at a time, while the rest of them weave back and forth in the background? They just bide their time looking menacing until they can get beaten up, one by one. More like *West Side Story* than real fighting, if you ask me.

Well, in this skit, they show such stock footage. Then the actors gather at the village with fake spears and arrows coming out of them. They huddle together and promise that next time they will attack the hero all together. They leave the village in a frenzy, but the exact same footage is shown once more. The actors come back beat up again and proclaim, "What did we say? All together! What did we do? One at a time." The cycle repeats.

I think we have all had the experience of having a heart-to-heart discussion with a teen or young adult and feeling certain that we've made a breakthrough. Maybe we are talking about limiting drug use or controlling tempers or doing better in school. The discussion is sincere, and we seem to be connecting. The young person nods in agreement. She provides examples of her own. She gets into the conversation. Everything about her body language signals that she gets it. Rather pleased with ourselves, we wax philosophical as we go to bed, thinking of all the other wonderful advice we can provide at another juncture. Oh, the hubris.

A day or two later, we find that the young person did exactly what we asked her not to do. She gets defensive. She justifies her behaviors. She now discounts your advice. Or, she may express remorse only to repeat the same lapse in judgment time and again.

I suppose we all do this to some degree, but why is it that young people in particular seem to so often? This is especially relevant in addiction, as the disease is marked by the tendency of the afflicted to do exactly what they shouldn't.

A great portion of this has to do with neurodevelopment. I'm going to give the most to-the-point and useful neurodevelopment explanation I can think of. Here goes:

Your brain consists of two kinds of basic matter, white matter and gray matter. Gray matter includes neurons, and the white matter is a network of myelinated axons (or coated nerve fibers) that facilitate transmission between neurons. Think of gray matter as the circuits on your computer and the white matter as the wires. For this discussion, it's that simple.

You may have heard that brains do not mature fully until the age of twenty-five or so. Actually, the gray matter in your brain grows in volume until puberty, at which time it starts to prune itself, if you will, as it matures. The white matter continues to grow for the first four decades of our lives, constantly reworking connections between neurons to some degree. When scientists say that your brain isn't mature until your mid-twenties, they mean that the prefrontal cortex, the part of your brain just behind your forehead and hairline, doesn't mature until then. I can explain further.

Your brain has two basic control centers: the limbic system and the prefrontal cortex. The first control center, the limbic system, is a primitive one. It exists under the shell of all the noodly cortices that we typically associate with brain imagery in popular media. It is a part of the brain that we have in common with many lower life forms. The limbic system includes structures such as the amygdala and hippocampus. Among other tasks, the limbic system helps us form memories, especially emotional memories. It helps to control motivation and fear and reward and feelings. The limbic system is instinctive. Animals that are driven mainly by the limbic system act based on their immediate needs or assessments of threat versus reward. The amygdala in particular is one of the reasons that we tend to remember emotionally significant moments, like fearful events or favorite holidays, as opposed to less emotionally significant content, like what we ate for breakfast three weeks ago.

Our brain's reward center, which is often talked about in addiction literature, also can be thought of as a part of this more primitive part of the brain. The nucleus accumbens is one of the regions often associated with addiction. Many, but not all, "addictive" chemicals (like cocaine or alcohol or nicotine) will in the end increase dopamine concentrations in the nucleus accumbens. Dopamine is the major neurotransmitter that our brain uses to signal reward. But the reward center isn't just about addiction. Basically, when we take in any rewarding stimuli, like good food, sex, or music, the reward center shoots out a little dopamine to tell us that what we experienced was good. Then the rest of our limbic system kicks into gear to make sure that we form a strong memory of this event. It's easy to imagine how this was helpful in "caveman days" when our ancestors happened to find a new source of food and subsequently formed a strong memory so as not to forget where they found it.

Addiction occurs in modern times when this primitive reward system is hijacked and recalibrated to demand a similar reward time and again by ingested chemicals or highly rewarding behaviors like gambling. Because of the reward involved and because of the memories associated with addiction, addiction is sometimes referred to as a relationship.

I employ this analogy often with kids. Addiction is an artificially induced love, in every sense of the word. It is a torrid love affair with a significant other with whom you have great chemistry, but it's an incredibly unhealthy relationship. This relationship, no matter how self-destructive, lives not just in our reward system, but in our memories. One of the reasons that there is no "cure" for addiction is because a person cannot forget about a significant former lover completely. There will be reminders and triggers, especially shortly after the breakup. Maybe it's music or the smell of their cologne or perfume, or a person who looks similar from behind. The triggers and memories can fire up years later in much the same way that we all sometimes think about former relationships despite a considerable passage of time. The best we can do is to move on from that relationship, replace it with a healthier relationship, and manage those falsely nostalgic memories.

Getting back on point, since we share the limbic system with lower life forms (such as rats), we can simulate addiction in the lab. That is how we know addiction is a real entity. It exists and can be reproduced. It does not require anyone's belief to exist, in much the same way that car accidents are very real regardless of whether anyone "believes" in them. In the lab, a scientist might stick a probe into the rat's brain, specifically where the reward circuitry lies. When the rat pushes a button or performs an activity that activates the probe, that reward center lights up, and the rat will forgo everything else to keep that feeling coming. Move that probe just a tiny bit away from the reward system, and the rat will stop its reward-seeking behaviors. That's how neurologically wired we are for addiction.

We humans have a well-developed second control system in the brain. This area is called the prefrontal cortex. It's basically a large chunk of the front two lobes of the brain. This noodly structure is more developed in humans than in other mammals. Its jobs are many. Think of it as the CEO of your brain. Baser passions and instincts (like fear) come in through the limbic system. The prefrontal cortex ultimately helps to control or suppress or redirect these instinctive responses (like rationalizing our fear). The prefrontal cortex allows us to sequence actions, stop and alternate tasks, and control our impulses and feelings, and it helps us organize. It may be responsible for a large measure of our personalities. It gives us our sense of working memory, which is like a temporarily accessible and easily maneuverable memory (for example, remembering a ten-digit code and holding the numbers in our minds short term). The prefrontal cortex does many other things as well, but basically it is supposed to override more primitive areas of the brain and provide us with sound judgment.

The problem is that in young people the limbic system develops much faster than the prefrontal cortex. When it comes to brain functions, instinctive traits and basic motor function develop before higher-level functions like planning or suppressing impulses as a result of this discrepancy. The discrepancy may also explain in part why teenagers are so prone to risk-taking and thrill-seeking behaviors.

So, in summary, a teenager's or young adult's prefrontal cortex is at war with the limbic system for ultimate control. In most cases, the prefrontal cortex wins out with maturity by a person's mid-twenties or so. Teenagers are actually just as bright as adults. If life were a multiple-choice test or even a hypothetical judgment test under calm conditions, teenagers would fare just as well as adults. But under pressure or emotional stress, their prefrontal cortices cannot consistently override what the limbic system desires. This is further complicated by addiction, which primes the limbic system to dominate the struggle.

This is why a calm teenager will sincerely internalize good advice from you but might let you down under pressure when an attractive interest offers them a drink or drugs. This is all the more reason not to rely on your intellect and philosophy as the

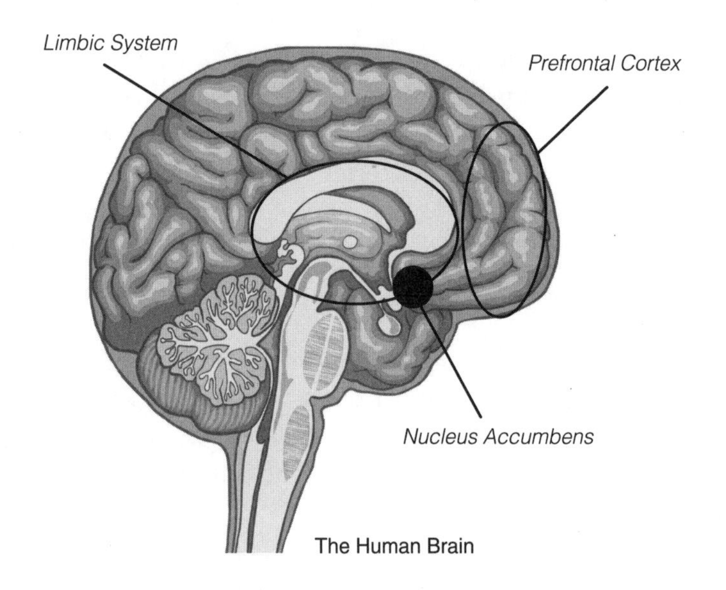

The Human Brain

main tool for reaching your son or daughter. Understand that teenagers will repeatedly make errors in judgment, especially when they aren't in a calm state of mind. This is why I have been asking you to build a culture based on leadership and emotional objectivity.

Bottom line: *Kids are smart but not necessarily wise. Don't place unfair expectations on their judgment and don't assume you have prevented all future problems with one good heart-to-heart.*

Chapter 25

Your Child Does Not Fit into a Bin—Keeping Diagnoses in Perspective

The medical community has come a long way in recognizing substance abuse and mental health problems as major public health issues. For example, we now know that cigarettes are the number one killer in the United States. Nearly 500,000 people die every year due to some complication from tobacco use, including, but not limited to, cancer or heart disease.

When the costs of lost productivity, legal problems, and health problems are added up for all substance-abuse-related matters, the Centers for Disease Control and Prevention (CDC) estimates that the United States, as a country, loses almost $500 billion each year due to chemical use.

Furthermore, the prescription drug epidemic is cited by some as the major health problem facing this country. The CDC reports that drug overdoses now eclipse motor vehicle accidents in the number of deaths caused.

Over the past few decades, these statistics prompted academics and clinicians and policy makers alike to standardize the way that we think about mental health and addiction problems. This effort has had its successes.

For one thing, the stigma that surrounds these problems—though still present—has lessened dramatically (even since my time in training, not too long ago). Addiction is now seen as a disease, not a character defect. I shudder to think about a time when addicts were shunned by the medical profession and labeled by churches and laypersons as morally compromised people. And I am moved by the compassion and progressive thinking of treatment organizations that give comfort and care to those who have nowhere else to turn.

In addition, our modern diagnostic assessments give us a powerful tool for making sense of mental health and addiction problems. Diagnoses help us group symptoms and their probable causes into clusters. They also help us standardize the way we talk to each other about problems with our health. We can gather statistics and research ailments that affect similar persons. All of this simply makes good sense, whether we're talking about physiologic diseases (such as pneumonia) or mental health issues (such as depression or anxiety).

In the mental health world, common causes for diagnoses are more difficult to establish. This is due, in part, to our limited understanding about how the brain actually works in psychological terms.

Nevertheless, we know these symptom sets for mental health issues do exist. Why? Because they span time and cultures. We can go through the annals of time and check the historical records—or visit remote cultures that have survived to the present day—and confirm the existence of problems with mental health and addiction. In fact, those problems look eerily similar to what we see today in developed countries such as the United States.

Diagnoses are useful. They give us a code. They make for efficient communication between the clinicians who treat people. The wrong diagnosis can lead to inaccurate treatment and unfortunate results. When it comes to mental health issues, a diagnosis is designed to describe what's going on with your child in a systematic and objective way.

Moreover, diagnoses help us think about a person's risk factors and zero in on effective treatments. Diagnoses can ensure that people aren't mistreated. And in the case of addicts, a diagnosis can help to rightfully ease much of the stigma and personal blame that come their way.

Difficulties arise, however, when we look at our children too narrowly through a diagnostic lens. The challenge becomes even greater when psychiatric problems occur at the same time as addiction—a situation that is often described as *co-occurring disorders*, *dual disorders*, or *dual diagnoses*.

Let me be clear: I am a believer in diagnostic approaches, imperfect as they are. On the other extreme are loose, "feel good" approaches to treating mental health problems that, despite their outward appeal, lack any solid grounding in science. I am not a fan of those inconsistent methods. That being said, let's proceed with the discussion.

Over two-thirds of young people with addiction have mental health issues. These issues occur at a significantly higher rate among younger people in treatment than among adults. If your teen or young adult has an addiction, chances are that he will have at least one corresponding mental health problem as well. Many kids have more than one. When a young person enters care, the presence of co-occurring disorders—dual diagnoses—is the rule and not the exception. For example, a child may be addicted to pain medication and cannabis, but may also have ADHD and anxiety. When informed parents research adequate treatment centers and clinics for their children, they look for centers where both psychiatric and mental health problems can be addressed simultaneously.

The term *dual diagnosis* has been around for at least a couple of decades and is often thrown around in the treatment community. As an aside, I have never really favored this term. It's not that the concept of dual diagnoses is completely inaccurate.

There's just something about it that suggests a double-barreled shotgun approach—as if there is nothing more in a child's profile. Somewhere between all the diagnoses, the child can get lost.

I also believe that the division between addiction and mental health diagnoses is unnecessary. Both addiction and psychiatric diagnoses have their origins in our neurology. Both manifest in our behavior. From this perspective, the differences are not profound.

In many ways, addiction is a mental health issue in and of itself. In fact, addiction is classified alongside every other psychiatric diagnosis in the *Diagnostic and Statistical Manual of Mental Disorders*, fourth edition, published by the American Psychiatric Association. This book is known as the DSM-IV. A fifth edition of the manual is due for release soon. Its definition of addiction may change slightly, but addiction's parallels to other mental health diagnoses will not.

In my estimation, the distinction between psychiatric and chemical dependency problems is probably political, meaning that traditionally, people with addiction didn't want to be seen as having mental health problems and vice versa. As an idea, the concept of dual diagnoses is well intentioned. Unfortunately, sometimes the focus on neatly packaged diagnoses is entirely too simplistic.

How do we individualize care when so many cases look so similar in terms of diagnosis? Let's be more specific about the limitations of the diagnostic approach.

First, *many kids do not fit diagnostic categories very well*. Making a diagnosis is like putting a square peg in a round hole. For example, I see many kids who have some mild features of autism, even though they don't meet the DSM-IV criteria for autism. Nonetheless, these kids are functionally impaired. The truth is, there are more "kinds" of kids than can be sorted and explained by any diagnostic model.

Second, *few young people with the same diagnoses are actually that much alike*. Every kid with depression and anxiety that I've treated has been unique. Sure, they all had similar symptoms and described their distress accordingly. Yet all these kids were different.

For example, one young man with generalized anxiety might worry about his future. Another might worry about getting diseases. And yet another might worry about his loved ones passing away. One young woman with depression may engage in cutting herself (self-injurious behavior). Another may restrict her food consumption but not to the point of having an eating disorder. The possible variations are endless. This reminds me of a line from *Hamlet*: "'There are more things in heaven and earth, Horatio, than are dreamt of in your philosophy.'"

Psychiatrists, psychologists, and other mental health professionals have responded to this shortcoming of "diagnoses" by coming up with approaches such as the *biopsychosocial model*. True to its name, this model suggests that biological, psychological, and social factors *all* play into an illness. And that's accurate, of course.

Truth be told, however, the biopsychosocial model is not always used by clinicians, like the people who are treating your child. And it can be difficult for parents to understand this model in theory, let alone apply it in daily life. Allow me to crystallize things a bit in the chapters that follow.

Bottom line: *Many of the young people that clinicians see for addiction look rather similar on paper. There's the drug use, of course. But often that comes with depression, anxiety, or both—along with ADHD and perhaps a number of traumatic experiences in the mix. If clinicians aren't careful about this complex reality, treatment becomes too standardized, and individual needs are lost in the shuffle.*

Chapter 26

Disease Process + Personal Factors = Holistic Care

Physiologic diseases—especially diseases like diabetes that are chronic or develop over a period of time—are best understood in the following way:

First, we consider the *disease process*. In the case of diabetes, this is high blood glucose and all of the biological changes related to it.

Second, we identify factors that contribute to the disease process (also called predispositions). Examples include

- a genetic vulnerability for developing an illness (such as an extensive family history of heart disease)
- how much the person exercises
- what kind of food the person eats
- how that person manages stress

For the sake of discussion, we can lump all of these together and call them *personal factors*.

The disease process and personal factors work together. For instance, people who are diagnosed with diabetes (a disease process) may not eat well (a personal factor). As a result, these people find it hard to regulate their blood sugars, even if they inject insulin or take other medications.

I talk about disease processes and personal factors for a reason—because *when we say addiction is a disease, we should mean it.* That is, we should think about psychiatric disease processes and addiction in the same way that we would think about diabetes.

Start with the *disease process* of addiction. A young person's brain—specifically, the reward circuitry—is altered to crave certain substances regardless of cost or consequence.

In addition, consider the personal factors. For example

- This young person's lifestyle, stress coping habits, personality, and genetics may indicate that she was vulnerable for addiction all along.
- A detailed family history might reveal that a number of grandparents and uncles and perhaps even a parent struggled with addiction at one point.
- The young person may have started to use substances at an early age, conferring high risk for developing addiction.
- The young person may have exhibited early behavioral or mental health problems.
- The young person might have maladaptive ways of dealing with stress and poor relationship management skills. (On the other hand, maybe she was sober for one year before she relapsed again, perhaps making her treatment outcome a bit more favorable.)

All of these personal factors lead to obstacles or benefits in treatment and shape the person's prognosis for recovery.

Now take another example—a young person with depression. The disease process of depression can be tricky to define in biological terms. Think of it as a constellation of symptoms that range from low mood to recurrent hopelessness and suicidal thoughts. These symptoms can be treated with therapy, medications, or both.

The personal factors in this child's depression might include

- chronic problems in regulating mood
- tendencies to seek isolation as a way to cope with stress
- a family history that involves several suicide attempts
- a sedentary lifestyle
- difficulty with making friends due to poor self-image

In both examples—addiction and depression—the disease process corresponds with diagnoses. And, we can respond to disease processes with evidenced-based treatments. For instance, we prescribe insulin for low blood glucose and blood pressure medications for hypertension. *Without careful attention to genetic and lifestyle factors, however, these disease processes can recur time and again.*

This seems so obvious. And it has huge implications.

In hospital settings, I have seen the distinction between disease process and personal factors avoided all too many times. Consider a typical scenario: A patient with congestive heart failure and high cholesterol is stabilized in the hospital after admission for shortness of breath. He is discharged with a large bag of medicines, even though he cannot pronounce the names of half of them.

By all measures, this man's condition is once again stable. He feels grateful. The team of physicians and nurses feel a certain accomplishment. Unbeknownst to them, the man returns to the hospital one month later when many of those clinicians have now rotated on to another medical service.

The problem here is that this patient's personal factors and other vulnerabilities were not adequately addressed during his first hospital admission.

Perhaps this man

- has a long history of taking medications incorrectly—or not taking them at all
- has transportation issues that make it hard for him to access a pharmacy for refills
- eats unhealthy processed foods high in fats
- leads a sedentary lifestyle, which renders medical treatments ineffective in the long run
- smokes cigarettes
- experiences high levels of stress and doesn't know how to cope with it
- struggles with depression due to a number of unforeseen setbacks in his life

Had these personal factors been identified and addressed, it's possible that this man's early return to the hospital could have been prevented.

Unfortunately, a similar scenario often unfolds in mental health treatment. In the chapters that follow, I'll explore this issue and revisit the distinction between disease processes and personal factors.

In essence, what I am asking you to do is to abide by the Serenity Prayer:

God, grant me the serenity
to accept the things I cannot change,
courage to change the things I can,
and wisdom to know the difference.

It's funny how well this prayer works. When it comes to addiction and psychiatric treatment, it reminds you to separate what you and your child *can* influence (personal factors) from what you and your child *cannot* influence (the disease process). Finding that balance is essential to keeping a healthy perspective.

Bottom line: *Disease process refers to the elements of a person's problem that can be addressed by clinicians, at least in part, as long as the person cooperates with treatment.*

Personal factors, on the other hand, are variables that clinicians cannot directly control. These factors can complicate treatment, render treatment ineffective, or make a person vulnerable to relapse.

Looking strictly at diagnoses and disease processes while ignoring personal factors can lead to ineffective care.

Chapter 27

Attribution in Mental Health Treatment

Mental health and addiction concepts create much stress for parents. They can be vague and inexact. Despite increased social acceptance, psychiatric and addiction issues are fraught with stigma. Even people who are free of this stigma can still have strong biases or opinions about these issues.

Why do we get so worked up about mental health treatment? In addition to the stigma and the less-than-precise nature of this field, there are even more fundamental factors at work. These include powerful sentiments that can divide the members of your family. The parents I speak to have different, but often equally emphatic, notions about what's going on with their child.

When seeking to understand a young person's addiction, some parents choose to see their kid primarily through the lens of mental health issues: *My child has always had low self-esteem and depression. I think that is why he self-medicated with drugs.*

Other parents are skeptical of mental health treatment. These parents might think that the diagnoses are feeble attempts to cover up a young person's poor judgments—a way for kids to avoid accountability: *I didn't raise my child this way. What she's doing is an offense to herself and our family's reputation.*

Some parents have a psychodynamic slant. This means they see addiction as a direct result of unresolved inner conflicts that, in turn, are influenced by certain past experiences, especially those that involved close family relationships: *Dad didn't attend Dan's soccer games, and the boy has always been bitter since. Alyssa has never been the same since that trauma (or divorce or bullying incident), though she won't admit it.*

Others see mental health as primarily a neurobiological problem in the brain: *Anthony had a great childhood. I just don't get why he went through this kind of change in his mind and body.*

The point is that addiction and mental health issues arouse strong sentiments in a way that few health issues do. Few people get equally heated about heart disease, for example. People often feel concerned about medical conditions, but rarely does the conversation get polarized and personal.

The domain of mental health—the world of thoughts, feelings, and behaviors—cuts deeply to our core. Mental health problems are largely about behavior. In the end, our behaviors say plenty about who we are, what we're thinking, and how we're feeling.

Talking about addiction and mental health leads us to reflect on our values, religious beliefs, and culturally accepted practices. And in facing a mental health diagnosis, we are forced to say something fundamentally honest about ourselves. Sometimes this brings forth epiphanies, wisdom, and reconciliation. At other times, the diagnosis leaves us naked and exposed, staring at reflections in the mirror that we struggle to accept.

Before we can really help our children in an objective way, we must admit our preconceived notions. And in order to do this, we must talk about two overlapping concepts: attribution and symbolism.

Let's tackle attribution first. Human beings have a natural and unquenchable need for making links between causes and effects: *I ate a sandwich before I was attacked by a shark while swimming in the ocean. I wonder if the sandwich had something to do with it?*

This is our need for attribution. Sometimes the search for causes, or attributions, is helpful. Yet the same need can also lead to stereotyping and every other false generalization that human beings make.

Once an attribution is made, the door is open for a host of distortions in thinking: *They should ban all sandwiches from the beach! The sandwich shop owners are responsible and must be stopped.* I've used analogies such as this to remove the emotional sting from some infamous attribution errors. You can use your imagination to do the same thing.

Now let's get back to mental health treatment. Suppose that a child blurts out impulsive statements in class. Forget about diagnoses for a second. Just think about how people might interpret such behavior:

- One teacher may decide that the child's behavior is completely voluntary, intended to gain favor from other students.
- Another might attribute the behavior to immaturity.
- Still another teacher might cut the child some slack, concluding that the child has ongoing stress at home and simply needs to vent.

These attributions are, in turn, founded on the teachers' individual life experiences, values, and belief systems:

- The teacher who interpreted the behaviors as strictly voluntary may be on a mission to correct a societal failure—that children are poorly instructed in manners at home.
- The teacher who attributed immaturity might automatically link child behavior to stages in growth and development.
- The teacher who cut the student some slack may have personally experienced a similar problem when he or she was young.

Can you see how our personal views alter our attributions? It works in a similar way with families who deal with a kid's addiction. A family with a long medical history of addiction could attribute their child's behavior to addiction without much difficulty. In contrast, a family without such a medical history can have a lot of difficulty with attributing anything to addiction.

Attribution suggests more than cause and effect. It also implies accountability. When young people have addiction and mental health problems, we not only want to know *why*—we want to know *who* or *what* is responsible. In other words, we can get overzealous in our pursuit for a "smoking gun."

Let me explain. Some parents are, at least initially, in denial about the degree of their child's drug use. The possibility of addiction shatters all their notions about how they see their children. Even parents who are aware of the drug use are frequently surprised by the full extent of it, or by the excessive and damaging behaviors that went along with the addiction.

Some of us want to preserve images of our children as they were in happier times, wholesome and undamaged. We might prefer to deny the presence of addiction. Or we might admit the addiction, but minimize its role in comparison to an overwhelming life event: *If only that car accident had never happened. If only her mother were still alive.* While such might be true in some cases, narrow interpretations can be detrimental to progress in addiction treatment.

On the other hand, some parents shift the burden of attribution to mental health problems instead of addiction. This blinds them to the truly manipulative and falsely pious nature of addiction-driven behavior.

Remember that it is common for addicts—without realizing it—to do whatever they can to sabotage care. Their brain simply demands that the ends justify the means. For this reason, addicts in treatment often carry on with a litany of complaints. They complain about withdrawal. They complain about insomnia.

They complain about anxiety and depression. They complain about antics of their peers in treatment and the quality of the staff. They might even complain about the food in the cafeteria. The possibilities are endless—and, believe me, I've heard them all. And even though these complaints might be legitimate, they can also be attempts to resist change.

If parents are misled by such false attributions, they can end up on a quixotic crusade for their child. They switch treatment centers and clinics, only to find that the complaints persist or evolve into new tirades. Eventually, no treatment center seems good enough. At some point, parents finally realize that addiction rather than mental health issues was driving their discontentment all along.

Others among us may react to the ways that a child's addiction injures us in a personal and emotional way. Imagine a depressed young man with addiction and truly manipulative behaviors. His parents may overreact to the manipulation and downplay his need for mental health treatment. They are shocked to find out later that his untreated use and low mood have led to suicidal thinking; but even then, it is natural for these parents to wonder if they are being gamed somehow.

Faced with such a situation, we may desire justice. Feeling betrayed, we may see our child as ungrateful and self-absorbed. We may have religious or cultural influences that emphasize personal responsibility. From this vantage point, any conversation about addiction as a disease seems like an excuse, and just about any psychiatric diagnosis looks like an alibi. (Sometimes diagnoses *are* used that way, as I'll explain in a later chapter.)

I totally understand where these parents are coming from. They have been lied to and stolen from. Perhaps their kid's addiction led to violence. The sheer number of such incidents and the havoc they create make it hard for parents to believe that they're really dealing with a disease.

In summary, parents may find mental health or addiction

more stigmatizing and will therefore emphasize one or the other. I generally find that parents prefer their children to have a mental health problem rather than an addiction. And this preference is more often expressed about girls. Why? Who knows?

I can't tell you the number of times a parent has told me, "I think it's mainly the depression and not the addiction we're dealing with." (In the previous sentence, you can substitute just about any other mental health diagnosis for the word *depression*.) But think about this for a minute. If someone is diagnosed with diabetes, high cholesterol, and high blood pressure, wouldn't it be silly to say, "I think it's mainly the cholesterol"?

Effective treatment means attending to all facets of a person's health at the same time. But for some reason, this perspective gets lost in the mental health world. When it comes to anything psychological, the pecking order of the attributions suddenly matters. One kind of problem has to be more important than the others. This is one of the reasons I do not like the term *dual diagnosis* or the artificial distinctions between addiction and mental health issues.

I must offer a caveat here: Though it's generally wise to treat mental health and addiction problems together, there are times when mental health issues can be treated *after* addiction treatment has begun. If a child has ADHD, for example, clinicians might wait until the child has some sober time before making that diagnosis.

On the other hand, it's rarely a good idea to treat mental health issues *before* addiction. Young people with addiction simply aren't themselves. Trying to do therapy while they are looking at the world through the lens of an addict is nearly impossible.

Underneath it all, our thirst for attribution is partly driven by another possibility. *When we apply cause-and-effect thinking to our kid's addiction, we might find that our families, our parenting methods, and ourselves are indicted.* While realizing that no parent is perfect, we might still fear that we did something to make the addiction worse.

Let's face it: For some parents, the thought of having a kid with addiction is highly inconvenient. It shakes the foundations of the family. It compromises "reputation." Parents fear that someone will look at their family as "dysfunctional" or secretive. Or, they take the diagnosis personally and start defending themselves from the accusation that they were "bad parents"—a notion that never needed to be entertained in the first place.

I have worked with families who for years sent their child only to a therapist while denying requests for a substance abuse assessment. Everyone, including the therapist, semiconsciously colluded to resist the inevitable conclusion—that the young person is an addict. When the kid steps forward with disclosures of addiction, they are shocked. Yet they shouldn't have been. They were blinded by their need for attribution.

Other parents are too damning of themselves. They take on too much responsibility: *If only we had gotten help for the anxiety earlier. If only we'd known the bullying was going on. If only I hadn't gotten depressed after losing my job.* This, too, is an extreme view, and is just as unhealthy.

When we find out that our children have an addiction, our broken hearts demand an explanation. We want to reconcile the addicted child we see before us with the child we fondly remember. We feel desperate for answers as we attempt to pick up the pieces of our shattered world. We start our journey for solace from this common place, but we fear making the journey alone. As Antoine de Saint-Exupéry notes in *The Little Prince*, "It is such a secret place, the land of tears."

I have incredible sympathy for all of the parents who embark on this journey. Do not be disheartened if you find that an example from this chapter (or from any other chapter in this book) seems to describe your family. You are not alone. Millions of families have gone through the same process. Millions have reacted with the same biases and distortions. It's time to end that cycle.

While coping with the enormous pressure of a kid with addiction, it is not your fault that you relied on certain core beliefs and familiar ways of handling stress. The addiction does not mean you are a bad parent. It does not mean you are uncaring. It does not mean you are closed-minded. The very fact that you are reading this book is a testament to your commitment and undying love.

Do you see how, in the previous paragraph, I avoided attribution with you? How liberating it is when we are allowed to entertain a multitude of possibilities—even conflicting ideas—without resorting to strict cause-and-effect thinking.

Bottom line: *When your child is in treatment, remember that the goal is for him or her to get well. This may require that you surrender long-held beliefs about how things are, should be, or came to be. And it takes a tremendous amount of courage to be this vulnerable.*

Chapter 28

Symbolism in Mental Health Treatment

Everything in mental health treatment—from diagnoses to medications—is rich with symbolism, and in a way that is unique among medical specialties. By *symbol*, I mean a term that evokes thoughts and feelings far beyond its literal definition. Symbols can work with our attribution bias to create a life story that is more palatable or consistent with our belief systems.

Symbols can benefit us. A diagnosis, for instance, offers answers to people who cannot explain what is happening to them. A diagnosis can provide hope when people see that others with the same problem can get well. A diagnosis reminds us that we are not alone, and that we don't have to seek treatment in secrecy or isolation. This is the positive aspect of symbolism in mental health.

For example, I've diagnosed teenagers with Asperger's syndrome who for years had no idea why they behaved the way they did and why they struggled socially. The diagnosis was a revelation to their parents as well. It gave family members a way to talk about their difficulties without the unbearable sentiments of shame and failure. Until they got the diagnosis, the parents thought they were doing something wrong, and the kids believed that their problems resulted from personal failures.

Similarly, kids with compulsive hand washing and germ phobias may feel relieved when they no longer have to hide their behaviors. A diagnosis of obsessive-compulsive disorder can open up a conversation about treatment and new possibilities for the future.

The concept of addiction as a disease has likewise restored dignity to millions of people who were judged, downtrodden, and ashamed. The disease concept softened society's view that all addicts were completely accountable for their behaviors. This concept garnered sympathy and forged a spirit of camaraderie and fellowship among people living with addiction.

On the other hand, diagnoses and treatments can also become symbolic in harmful ways. For instance

- People can be grouped on the basis of a diagnosis and become victims of stigma: *Oh, that girl has borderline personality disorder, you know.*
- A diagnosis can be seen as a curse or an accusation of personal weakness, leading to denial: *I don't have any mental health issues; I don't want to talk to anyone about it.*
- Some kids actually see their diagnosis as a badge of honor—a way to validate their suffering: *I didn't know that this apathy and hopelessness I felt was called depression.* That's *why I am the way I am.* Sometimes though, this can go too far and become an excuse as well. *The only reason I didn't do well in class is because of my ADHD.*

Uncritical acceptance of a diagnosis can also be used to lower expectations of people (just as denial of a diagnosis can artificially raise expectations about what people can do without treatment). In effect, the diagnosis or symptom set keeps people stuck. The basic premise is this: If an obstacle is large enough and seemingly impossible to overcome, then there's no need for a full and brave effort.

Consider the kid who says, "I'm so depressed I can't do anything. Life seems so hopeless now." Is this depression being undertreated? Maybe not. If we take symbolism into account, we might discover a young person who's resisting change. It might be easier for kids to say that depression prevents them from getting work done than it is to admit that they feel overwhelmed by the journey ahead of them in treatment.

This is *not* to say that depression is a fiction. It simply means that a diagnosis or list of symptoms can sometimes be used to explain kids' distress in a way that holds them back.

Chronic pain is another complicated issue where symbolism can take hold of everyone involved. Sometimes there are very real reasons for the pain; at other times, no medical cause is found. In either event, the pain might be more than it appears. Pain can be a symbol of disability. It can represent a child's powerlessness in life and justify her lack of effort in school. Pain can encapsulate all the unfairness of life and reinforce a hopeless outlook. And due to the effects of symbolism, a child might find it more acceptable to express physical pain than anxiety or depression. The child's belief system can render physical pain as acceptable and mental health diagnoses as clear signs of a weak will.

I see many kids with just this kind of issue. They sometimes over-report mental health problems, and not because they want to make excuses. (The word *excuse* implies a rather conscious, calculated, and deliberate maneuver.) They over-report mental health symptoms because they want a palatable answer, or because their ego cannot bear a frontal assault on all their problems. A skilled clinician will be able to navigate through this dilemma while making sure the young person feels supported.

To further explain the potential pitfalls of symbolism, let me offer an analogy. Imagine a society in which the inability to run quickly is treated as a disease—*inefficient locomotion syndrome*. Nothing is physically "wrong" with people who are diagnosed with inefficient locomotion syndrome. They just run slowly.

Now, suppose that a group of kids is diagnosed with this disease—one that is both unfortunate and possibly fatal (that is, if you're being chased by a tiger or raging bull). Do we let these kids take it easy and avoid physical activity? Of course not. We encourage them to train harder at running and work up to the very limits of their ability. The diagnosis prevents us from seeing a lack of speed on foot as "laziness" and from blaming the kids for their corrupt moral character. At the same time, we don't let these kids succumb to their predisposition. We don't want their condition to deteriorate even further due to a lack of exercise.

If we aren't careful, diagnoses can turn someone into the Incredible Hulk, or a person resigned to having little control over his or her psychology. The Incredible Hulk is the legendary comic book and television character who once said, "You're making me angry. You wouldn't like me when I'm angry." We start walking on eggshells around our children, excusing every behavior and indulging every request for fear of making things worse.

At Hazelden, I see kids who have been diagnosed with almost everything in the book prior to admission. They enter treatment with a litany of complaints and sometimes with too many medications. Over time, these kids come to terms with their need for symbolism and attribution. They start to "own" their diagnosis and set aside their search for simplistic answers. Eventually, they leave treatment on fewer medications, with less suffering, and with a clearer understanding of the challenges that face them.

Like the Serenity Prayer says, these kids learn to control the things they can and let go of the things they cannot. There is such profound wisdom in that simple language.

Bottom line: *There are many children with developmental disabilities and serious mental health issues. We clinicians do what we can to maximize what these kids can do for themselves. We encourage their self-actualization while helping them find a balance between what they can control and what they cannot.*

Chapter 29

Drugs Are Not Just Drugs—Attribution and Symbolism Regarding Medication

Now let's talk about one of the most polarizing aspects of mental health care—medications. In this chapter, we'll discover how attribution and symbolism create unnecessary dilemmas in this aspect of treatment.

To begin, let me take another opportunity to point out the dangers of jargon: Drugs are not just drugs. That is, all drugs are not created equal. Yes, they are all chemicals that work on the brain, body, or both. But there are stark differences between two types of drugs.

The first includes potentially addictive drugs, defined in part by a rapid rise in blood levels of the chemical within a short time after ingestion. Nicotine in cigarettes is an example.

The second type of drug is potentially less addictive. These take more time to work—for example, antidepressants.

Some people oppose medications because they don't want to substitute their "drugs" with other "drugs." That is their right, but they are misusing terms. To avoid such confusion, I will use the term *medication* when referring to nonaddictive chemicals.

In the previous chapter, I explored the symbolism of diagnoses. Treatments can have inherent symbolism as well. Let's use diabetes as an example: A young girl abhors her daily insulin shots. They symbolize a part of herself she does not like. The shots might remind her of her own mortality. In her mind, they may also represent her parents' control of her. These are all potent examples of attribution and symbolism, and they could prevent her from complying with her treatment plan.

Here we need to revisit our previous discussion about disease processes and personal factors (see chapter 26: "Disease Process + Personal Factors = Holistic Care"). Remember that with any disease, we need to separate the disease process itself (such as low mood or high blood pressure) from the personal factors (genetics, personality, diet, exercise, uncontrollable circumstances, and the like). There is a reason I want you to look at mental health and addiction this way.

When it comes to treating a mental health issue, taking medications is like playing a sport with good equipment. Even when you own top-notch equipment, your skills are still important. For example, you can have the best baseball bat in the world and still strike out every time. You still have to practice. You still have to play the game. And you still need fair expectations for what equipment really can do to improve your performance.

So it is with treatment, including medication. Treatment often calls for more than medication. If someone's blood pressure is a bit high, for example, this person's genetics and risk for other diseases will be taken into account. Also, she will be asked to change her personal factors. This usually means eating less salt, exercising more, and losing weight. If those changes are ineffective over a number of visits, then the doctor will prescribe medication to bring the blood pressure numbers down.

Now, remember what this medication can do. It can save wear on the person's cardiovascular system and organs. It may even prolong her life. But the medications will not cause the person to eat better, exercise, or control her anger. Nor will medication change the person's family history of heart disease.

It seems so simple to remember these facts when it comes

to treating a condition such as high blood pressure. Why is it so hard for us to think this way when it comes to psychiatric medications? Again, it is all about attribution and symbolism.

Medications treat symptoms within the disease process. They can reduce the effects of personal factors, though they do not often directly change them. For example, medication can change personal factors such as a person's natural predisposition for irritable moods. But it does this by affecting the biological side of the spectrum.

Consider this example as a best-case scenario for medications: A young woman with social anxiety takes fluoxetine (Prozac) for a time. After a few weeks, she starts to feel better and begins talking in groups with greater confidence. These results build momentum over time, and after a year she slowly comes off the medicine. At that point, her anxiety is temporarily worse, but she copes with it by relying on all of the skills she learned in therapy and the confidence she developed. In the long run, she does fine without medications.

This example reminds us that young people with mental health problems often need therapy as well as medication. *Therapy*, broadly defined, is that which helps address the personal factors in a young person's clinical profile. This, in turn, can help the disease process.

The way that medications and therapy work together is similar to the way a transcontinental railroad is built. There's a construction crew laying tracks at one end of the continent and another crew at the other end. Eventually, the two crews meet in the middle of the country and connect the separate lines of tracks.

In a similar way, medications work from the disease end of the treatment spectrum, and therapy works from the personal end. People diagnosed with depression, for instance, can feel less irritable by taking medication. But that's just one line of the railroad. They need to change their personal factors—beliefs and behaviors—as well. They need to learn how to manage their emotional responses. They need to learn how to set healthy boundaries in relationships. They may need to exercise more. They need to address the genetic predisposition that makes them feel persecuted so easily. Doing all of the above in concert may improve their prognosis more than adherence to a more narrow treatment path.

Bottom line: *Medications won't automatically make addiction, depression, anxiety, or any other diagnosis suddenly disappear. The problem has many dimensions—and so does the solution. Medications, therapy, self-care, and self-help group membership all work together. That's what holistic treatment is all about.*

Chapter 30

Medications Don't Punch Back—Keeping Fair Expectations for Treatment

Although medications can be highly effective, we are still an overdiagnosed, overtherapized, and overmedicated society. This trend arises not because of a flaw in diagnoses or therapy or medications themselves, but rather because of how we often digest and use these terms. If you think about it, you'll see that these trends arise from our need for attribution and symbolism.

There are two major errors in much of our thinking about treatment. The first error occurs when medications represent more than they should. The second occurs when an unnecessary conflict is created between medications and other forms of therapy. I'll explore the first error here and save the second one for the next chapter.

Because of our established struggles with attribution, we sometimes want to find a third party we can hold accountable for a problem—preferably a party that will not punch back. This often happens during discussions about politics where the "bad guy" becomes "the government" or "our secular society," as if those vast aggregations of people somehow plan all their movements in concert. In the mental health and addiction arena, the third party can be a diagnosis, a medication, or a life event that no one could control.

When something goes wrong in substance abuse treatment, the first question I often get from parents and kids is "Was it the medication?" Another common question is whether they were on the "right" medications. These questions are legitimate, but we have to take a balanced approach.

In short, we need to reflect on the fact that *we demand more from psychiatric medications than any other treatment*. This is partly due to false advertising and aggressive promotion of medications by pharmaceutical companies.

It's also due to the stigma surrounding psychiatric medications. There are several reasons for this stigma. These medications, especially antipsychotics, can have big-time side effects. Even antidepressants can have emotional side effects, including suicidal thoughts. Even without side effects, the thought of young people needing any kind of medication doesn't sit well with people in an ideal world, and that is completely understandable. We need to prescribe these medications judiciously, with a clear purpose, and that often is not the case.

However, prevalence of negative side effects from psychiatric medications is far lower than what many parents think. Also, nonpsychiatric medications that raise similar concerns don't carry the same stigma. For example, antibiotics can cause a life-threatening rash called Stevens-Johnson syndrome. And some medications for the treatment of seizures may also cause suicidal thoughts. So can several of the medications for acne.

My point is that the ratios of benefits to risks with psychiatric medications are not necessarily appreciably different than the benefit-risk ratios for other kinds of medications. Yet people somehow see psychiatric medications as different in kind.

Consider an example that's typical of what I see. A young man in chemical dependency treatment has high levels of anxiety and depression. He struggles with chronic low self-esteem. And even before he used drugs, he had a habit of responding poorly to stress—for instance, he'd have a meltdown in class when a difficult academic project was due. As he got older, he started to contemplate suicide whenever he felt overwhelmed, which unfortunately was too often. He last thought of suicide one month ago, when his girlfriend of two years broke up with him.

This young man failed all lower levels of care, including outpatient and intensive outpatient treatment. He is now in residential care and feels unsure about how long he can stay sober. His counselor recommends more treatment at a halfway home after he is done with his current schedule of residential treatment. He doesn't like this idea because it will mean he cannot go home. He's had an argument with a peer who challenged his ambivalence. And he feels stressed because family meetings with parents have been heated. He recently got a prescription for an antidepressant, and he has been on it for approximately a week.

One day he decides to call his ex-girlfriend and finds out that she has moved on, so to speak. After this call, he reports feeling suicidal and says that he does not want to be in treatment at all.

This young man had led his parents to believe that he was "serious about getting sober this time." Now the parents have big doubts. They wonder if he is feeling suicidal because of his medication—or if his lack of commitment to treatment is due to the dosage or brand of the antidepressant.

To be fair to the parents, they don't have all the details. They don't live at the treatment center with him. They don't know about the argument with his peer or the call to his ex-girlfriend. And, to some degree, their concerns about the medication could even be valid.

What stands out to me time and again, however, is how quickly the conversation turns to medications. Maybe it is a byproduct of our litigious age and scare tactics used by malpractice lawyers. Who knows? But if medications are implicated so quickly, think about what this means for our young man. What does it say about his willingness to be accountable for his recovery or his ambivalence about treatment?

Again, let's think through some comparisons. Medically obese people with poor diet and exercise habits cannot blame their medicines for failing to lower their blood pressure. These folks are doing nothing to change their personal factors. Likewise, people with heart disease who have little regard for the role their personal factors play should not blame their cholesterol medicines when they have a heart attack. Again, the problem isn't whether medications can cause adverse effects at times. The problem is the disproportionate symbolism and attribution given to medications and all of the false expectations that come with them. Few people would make such errors in the way we think about most diseases. But when we enter the world of psychiatry and psychology, we do it most of the time.

Sometimes I feel forced to act conservatively and will discontinue a medicine that might be helpful when the finger pointing starts—defensive medicine at its finest. I know that this creates challenges. Some of these kids may need medication down the road. Based on a couple of weeks of therapy alone, it's hard for them to change beliefs and behaviors that took years to put in place. Yet I am compelled to stop the medicine because the symbolism and attribution given to a form of treatment that cannot talk back have already cast a decision for those involved.

Fortunately, in most situations, such as the one involving the young man I just described, I can show the family that his tendency to feel overwhelmed and suicidal under pressure was set in motion long before any antidepressant took the fall. Later on in treatment, this young man may face a similar crisis without medication and finally understand what is going on.

Sometimes the symbolism and attribution surrounding psychiatric medications swing to the other extreme. This happens when people overestimate the positive benefits of medication. I cannot tell you the number of times a young person has reported to me that "the pills really helped"—when it was still too early for the medication to take effect. Given what I know about how long it takes for certain medications to work and what changes we can expect them to make, I often find myself saying to kids: "The improvement was due to you, not the medicine."

Some kids in treatment are convinced that medications are *the* answer for them. Sometimes this is true, but often they are surprised to find out that they can do more with less. Generally, I find these young clients to be anxious, avoidant, or otherwise searching for a single solution to their distress. When clinicians don't pick up on this tendency, they risk polypharmacy—prescribing too many medications.

When I was in medical training, I was taught to look for "horses before zebras." In other words, we want to look at more common factors before the less common ones, while keeping an eye out for the rare event. Every good physician I know operates from this principle. The point is that we must be objective and balanced as much as possible.

Medications should be used with a purpose. This means admitting to our biases about addiction and mental health, giving them an audience, and keeping them in check. Remember that medications will never punch back when you accuse them.

Bottom line: *We need to make sure that we view psychiatric medications like we view antibiotics, insulin, or cholesterol medications. Avoid expecting more of any treatment than it can actually deliver.*

Chapter 31

Medication versus Other Treatments—Why the Conflict?

Another common error in thinking about mental health and addiction is the tendency to see medications and other treatments as rivals.

As I explained in the previous chapter, many people have a negative gut reaction to the whole topic of medications. Often these people see therapy as a better alternative. Therapy quickly becomes "good" and manufactured pills "bad." That leads to an all-or-none choice between medications and therapy that I find completely unnecessary.

Remember that therapy is not without hazards. When done poorly, in fact, *therapy can actually cause harm*. Poor boundaries, unreliable methods, and inappropriate messages are just the start. Just as some treatment centers do better at treating chemical dependency than others, some therapists provide better therapy. Some kids go to poor treatment centers and come out as worse addicts. And, like any professional, some therapists are better than others.

Our errors in thinking here parallel what we see in food advertising, which is laden with jargon—*natural*, *light*, *local*, *multigrain*, and the like. These terms are used with a kind of liberty that is misleading.

In a similar vein, I have talked to many kids who say that they prefer "natural" drugs like cannabis. Think about that for a second, however. There are many "natural" things that aren't good for you. Certain plants and fungi are incredibly poisonous, but certainly natural. Other "natural" elements in our bodies can become very toxic at higher-than-normal concentrations (iron, for example).

Therapy is often endorsed—and pharmaceuticals are often dismissed—with a similar kind of bias about what's more natural. The story line is that medication is synthesized by "greedy" and "heartless" corporations who push their products on common folks. Unfortunately, there is some truth to this. The pharmaceutical industry wields a double-edged sword, offering the good with the bad. What we need to think carefully about, though, is the proportion of good to bad.

I want to be fair here. Therapy is incredibly helpful if done well. It is the means through which I address the personal factors that contribute to a young person's addiction and mental health problems. This is something that medications cannot do directly.

In many situations, I actually recommend that a person try therapy *before* medications, just as I might recommend a person with borderline high blood pressure start exercising first. Again, I am using the word *therapy*, in a broad sense, as any form of talk therapy in group or individual settings, or even some forms of self-help (like meditation).

Additionally, a young person may prefer therapy over medications for severe anxiety or depression, despite the common advice to get both forms of treatment at the same time. This preference has roots in fears about side effects or beliefs that medications in general are overprescribed. For some kids, the choice of therapy also becomes a statement of autonomy: *As much as I can, I'm going to get better on my own*. This is a noble intent, to be sure, though in some situations it can be unwise.

At the other end of the spectrum are people who want a "pill" for everything. Again, these folks might have artificially high expectations for medication. And some kids want to hold medications accountable for their treatment so that they are relieved of personal responsibility for their role in recovery.

At times, mental health professionals and chemical dependency counselors contribute to the needless rivalry between treatment options by narrowing the scope of the problem unnecessarily or prioritizing the wrong issues first. This happens when clinicians

- unfairly attribute a child's problems to poor parenting, while failing to recognize the manipulative behaviors of an addict
- reinforce false beliefs that have to be undone later on (*It's all the fault of that kid who bullied you in fourth grade.*)
- place a higher priority on establishing rapport—getting clients to like them—than on doing what will actually help clients most in the long run
- share in the child's delusion that he can control his drug use when the presence of addiction is clear to everyone in the family
- filter their treatment through their specialty—for example, when a therapist who specializes in trauma digs into a child's past, searching for a traumatic event to the point of absurdity while ignoring the ongoing drug use

I have pretty much seen it all. Clinicians fall prey to attribution and symbolism errors because we, too, are human.

When people try their best to control their blood sugar levels with diet and experience no success, we don't blame them for taking a medicine. But when it comes to mental health treatment, we start drawing division lines. Some parents refuse medication for their children no matter what. Others are too impatient with therapy and demand medications too soon.

It's our job to check our biases at the door and examine why we feel so strongly about treatment options. Then we can make more objective decisions about what our children need.

Bottom line: *Attribution and symbolism drive some families toward one form of treatment versus another. Just as we need to evaluate mental health problems and drug problems together, we must be careful not to jump to conclusions about which treatments are best for our child's recovery.*

Chapter 32

The "Chicken or the Egg" Dilemma—Giving Up the Desire for a Linear Story Line

A family is involved in a car accident. Though they are shaken, everyone emerges from the experience safely. Hours later, they get into a discussion about what happened. It is clear that everyone in the family has a different opinion on why the accident happened and how it unfolded.

Dad believes that the tires were old.

Mom thinks that the roads were unsafe due to the weather.

Their teenager chimes in about the other driver talking on the cell phone and not paying attention.

In many ways, this is how events unfold in life. When something happens, we notice different things about it. We have unique takes on what transpired and what the important variables were. Many of our viewpoints can be valid and can even coexist.

Even so, we often want a more linear story line: First, we forgot to replace the tires. Then it rained and the roads got wet. And then the other driver answered her cell phone. That's how the accident *really* happened.

This reminds me of the so-called butterfly effect: A butterfly flaps its wings in a remote forest, creating tiny shifts in wind currents. This, in turn, triggers a series of meteorological events that gradually increase in magnitude until they eventually result in a hurricane. In other words, a minor event at one point in the past becomes the crux of a major event down the road. This is good stuff for philosophers and movie scriptwriters. But it's bad stuff for mental health and addiction treatment.

Addiction is complicated. It's composed of many factors—it's *multifactorial.* There are genetic risk factors. There are environmental risk factors. People with addiction can put themselves at high risk for tragic events. Addicts can be victims *and* antagonists, depending on the situation. For all these reasons, trying to create a straightforward plot line that explains how and why a young person became addicted is difficult, if not impossible. We can often benefit by giving up the search for what happened first—the addiction, the depression, the anxiety, the ADHD diagnosis, the bipolar disorder, the trauma, or whatever.

Understandably, parents often find this hard to accept. They want to find *the* reason that their child ended up addicted and in treatment. "We had a great kid," they say, "and then all this stuff happened." These parents want to connect the dots and fill the gaps, emerging with a solid story—a plot line that reveals *the* cause of their child's addiction.

Well, I think we all want to find *the* cause in such situations. We want some kind of accountability. But sometimes life is just messier than that—especially with a mental health issue or addiction that develops over many years.

If a company fails, what's the one thing that led to it? Is it the product they launched? Is it their awful CEO? Was it the changing economy? Well, perhaps it was all those things—and more. Maybe it's even possible to create several different narratives about what started the downhill slide. I see a similar phenomenon when kids develop issues that land them in treatment. A lot of variables need to be addressed. If you start putting too much weight on one factor versus another, you run into problems.

When people engage in telling their stories in therapy, they need to remember this: Therapy is a way of lining up one's ducks in a row in a way that makes sense for you. The narratives told and validated in therapy are partly factual and partly emotional. They are not court-of-law truth. The story lines that we learn to tell about ourselves can be useful, consistent, and plausible—but not necessarily the absolute truth. Any story is just one way to look at life that has meaning for the person in treatment. The plot line gets them from one place to another, clinically speaking. It helps them make peace with their past and gain hope for their future.

Therapy, then, is fundamentally open. Despite this fact, parents, patients, and clinicians can easily become vested in a rigid and linear narrative. And such narratives can be incredibly dangerous.

When teenagers come into treatment and are diagnosed with depression, their parents often ask me, "What came first? My kid was depressed, so he started self-medicating, right?" Or, "She was addicted, so then she became depressed, right?"

These are seemingly harmless questions, but they are loaded. I don't mean to be insensitive, but they remind me of the old conundrum of deciding which came first—the chicken or the egg?

Why do we default to a chicken-or-egg discussion when it comes to addiction and mental health? Thinking in those terms leads to several problems. Once again, we run into assumptions about attribution. We fear that we might be partially responsible for our children's addiction. Or, if we are not, we want to know what changed our children so dramatically. We assume that we can do something to rectify the situation if only we know the root cause. This thinking may or may not be realistic.

Stories that are too linear and rigid leave parents vulnerable for exploitation: *You hit me that one time when I was younger, so it's your fault that I'm screwed up.* Filtered through the beliefs and behaviors of an addict, this can translate to *I am going to use my resentments against you so that I don't have to change.*

Now, most young people are not this blatantly rigid about their life story. Yet, it's easy to see how a client who thinks this way might be hard to work with in treatment. When the narrative gets rigid, some parties become more accountable than others. If clinicians aren't careful, they can let the child's now-diminished accountability undermine the kind of changes that are necessary for recovery. Or addicted young people will repeatedly use their story as a tag line whenever they feel like they are losing leverage in a conversation. "I blame you for cheating on Mom. If you didn't get divorced, I wouldn't be so angry, and maybe I wouldn't use," or "How can you expect *me* to change after you've hurt me so much over the years?"

Another problem with rigid narratives relates to insight—psychological self-knowledge. Insight alone has never led to recovery. *There's a huge difference between knowing and accepting*, as we have established. Knowing is based on fact. Acceptance is knowledge plus a duty or commitment to do something about it. Gaining insight and establishing what "really happened"—in and of themselves—might not lead kids to make real changes in beliefs and behaviors that lead to favorable treatment results. (For more on this, see chapter 8: "The Difference between Knowing and Accepting.")

Think about it. Lots of people know they are obese and need to lose weight, for example. Do they always follow through with changes in diet and exercise? No. It works the same way in mental health and addiction treatment. The scientific literature has established that insight alone doesn't significantly boost rates of sobriety. Insight might be helpful in framing a problem properly. Depending on the situation, insight might be *necessary*. But it certainly is not *sufficient*. So even in situations where a rigid and linear narrative sounds correct, it may not be as helpful as we might expect.

Bottom line: *Sometimes linear causality is a reality. But in most aspects of our lives, especially with conditions that develop over a period of years, life is multifactorial. A lot of things have to happen in order to produce a particular outcome. Better to surrender the need for explanations about what happened in the past and do what's needed for your child's recovery in the present. There will be ample time to make amends, if necessary, when the timing is right.*

Chapter 33

Going Beyond Split Attribution—the Power of *And* Statements

Sometimes I ask people to free associate—to speak whatever comes to mind in response to a particular term or phrase. When I say *blond*, some people say *dumb*. When I say *nerdy*, they say *weak*. This little experiment opens a window to the polarizing aspect of our minds—the tendency to think in terms of opposites.

Our minds naturally ascribe rather polarizing attributes to people: *blond* versus *smart*, *nerdy* versus *strong*. The associations that pop into our heads turn people into predictable, one-dimensional beings. Our thinking takes on a "seesaw" quality. We see this, for example, in our society's fascination with celebrities. We build them up with uncritical adoration. Then we bring them down with scandal, or we ascribe personality traits even though we know nothing about them personally ("He's a spoiled celebrity"; "She's a terrible mother"). I don't know why we do this, but we do. I suppose it's a kind of stereotyping, but *stereotype* is too broad a term. Let's call it *split attribution* instead. The people who feed us our daily news are often guilty of split attribution.

We can even succumb to split attribution when trauma is involved. The victim is frequently imbued with more wholesome or innocent qualities; the antagonist is simply seen as evil. In reality, though, people who have been abused can abuse others;

kids who are bullied can later bully others. Bad things happen to good people and not-so-good people, and sometimes good people do bad things.

Again, we need a balanced message, especially given the amount of manipulation that takes place in addiction. How do we achieve this balance? How do we support and comfort troubled individuals—*and* ask them to embrace their accountability?

At Hazelden, I tell young people that recovery is letting go of one rope you cannot control in order to grab one that you can. Paradoxically, this means gaining power in your life by sacrificing the effort to control something that you are powerless over anyway. It's the essence of the Serenity Prayer. Or, to use another metaphor, it's putting your psychological funds into something that will bear fruit and admitting that your current investments are out of control.

The solution to split attribution—and the path to having a balanced discussion—is straightforward. I call it "the *and* statement." This simply means that we use the word *and* whenever we feel like using the word *but*. The word *but* suggests that everything in a sentence prior to that point is invalid. "I think you are a nice kid, but. . . ." In contrast, *and* allows for two different ideas to coexist. (Up to this point I haven't used *and* statements because you might have questioned my strange writing style.)

Let's put this technique into action. We can say that

- A kid was bullied throughout his life—*and* he has some inherent deficits when it comes to keeping friends.
- A young adult grew up with verbally abusive parents—*and* he has difficulty in controlling his emotions.
- A young woman experienced horrendous sexual trauma—*and* she can take on increasing accountability in her addiction.

This technique allows you to say that a number of bad things happened in your life—*and* it is still your life to live.

Again, timing is critical. Before using *and* statements, I first make sure that kids feel heard and supported. Once that is done, the *and* statement can help all of us withhold judgment. It allows us to entertain conflicting ideas without having to come up with a solution right away. It gives people space while gently setting limits.

The *and* statement will allow you as a parent to apologize for any wrongdoing in the past when the time is appropriate while still maintaining boundaries: *I am sorry I wasn't there for you*, and *this is what I have to do for you now*. This is so much more liberating than *I feel guilty about what I did* or *I should have done more*, which in turn leads to *I'm not sure what I should do next*.

The beauty of working with young people is the presence of hope. Their life stories have not been written in stone. A seventeen-year-old can learn to reframe her story in a way that maximizes sympathy from caregivers *and* creates accountability for recovery. How great it is to work with a young person when the narrative is evolving. It's not at the final draft. Without too much difficulty, kids in recovery can move from *It was my mother's fault* to *I was deeply hurt*, and *I'm responsible for changing my behavior*.

In contrast, the older the client, the more careful we have to be about reframing narratives. Older adults may have lost jobs. They may have been through chaotic divorces. And they may have unresolved conflicts. Adults, too, need to make peace with their life story, but it is more likely that they will be much more guarded about how things really went down. Sometimes the symbolism and attribution elements are just too hardwired.

Bottom line: *Use an* and *statement the next time you feel a strong pull toward a linear narrative, or whenever you find yourself saying* but *way too much. You'll be surprised at the emotional balance it gives. Using* and *statements offers an opportunity to validate your kid's feelings while not giving ground to addictive behaviors. Your child will feel heard and respect your boundaries all the more.*

Chapter 34

The Potential Perils of Digging Up the Past

In this chapter, I'd like to put our desire for a linear story line into a larger context. From time to time, I give talks to clinicians where I present a patient case (altered to protect privacy, of course). Following the Socratic method (a method of teaching named for the philosopher Socrates), I ask a series of questions to encourage discussion about ways to assess and treat the patient.

When the clinicians get stumped, one of the first questions they ask is: *What happened in the child's past?*

This question might be right on track. But what's more relevant is that we go there so quickly. Why do we assume that some seminal event from early childhood caused a child's problems?

This is analogous to physicians jumping to the same diagnosis every time they see someone who's sick: *Is it cancer?* Maybe it truly *is* cancer, but what's more interesting is why this word comes up first.

Western psychology and psychiatry have long been slanted toward psychodynamic principles—that is, attempts to understand inner conflicts we might not be readily aware of. In practice, this almost always deals with current problems by digging up events from the past, as a way to say that those events may have impacted us more than we thought. As I mentioned earlier, these principles often suggest that emotional problems stem from unconscious conflicts in our psyche. More often than not, these conflicts originate in the family, especially from our relationships with parents and significant others.

Speaking in historical terms, Freud's psychodynamic principles did much to encourage intellectual discourse on all matters of the mind. His theories, whether completely accurate or not, have influenced everything from clinical practice to plots in films and novels. And though mental health professionals have moved away from psychodynamic principles, we still use psychodynamic jargon in everyday life.

My point is simply that psychodynamics went too far. It got to the point where every kid's problem was traced back to what happened in the family, especially during early interactions with parents. (You've probably seen a Woody Allen movie or two based on this premise.) Sure, there are definitely parents who add to their child's misery; some parents are chiefly responsible. The casualty of our psychodynamic bias, however, was that so many less-than-perfect but good parents were unfairly blamed for messing up their children.

This led to a backlash, of course. Who wants to take their child in for treatment and end up with sole responsibility for the problem? Resistance to this scenario helped to promote biological psychiatry, where the culprit switched from "mom issues" or "dad issues" to the kid's neurochemistry. It could be argued that this trend of biological psychiatry has gone way too far as well in the opposite extreme.

Today, the psychodynamic influence is coming back around. Watch almost any documentary about addiction, and you'll see it. The narrative is no longer as much about parental dynamics, however. Instead, the story revolves around the idea that the person in question became addicted because of something that happened to him or her in the past.

A while back, I read about a study done by researchers who

took parents of kids with mental health issues, broke the parents into groups defined by ethnicity, and then gave them a survey.[2] The researchers asked the parents: Why do you think your child has problems?

Compared to ethnic minority parents, Caucasian parents were much more likely to believe that their child's mental health problems stemmed from some problem in the family. Put another way, African American, Latino, and Asian American families did not subscribe to the Western psychological explanations for their child's troubles in the same way that Caucasian families did. It is clear from this study that not all ethnic groups and cultures share a psychodynamic bias that sends them looking for "what happened to you in your family."

Again, "lining up your ducks"—creating therapeutic narratives about our past—can be useful. These narratives may yield profound symbols of recurring themes in our lives. The ways we view our past relationships might not be the truth, but these viewpoints can help us move forward. However, I still see too many mental health and addiction professionals relying on the "what happened in your past" angle without a clear rationale.

Digging up the past is an intuitive approach, for sure. It is also good for establishing rapport (helping the client to trust the therapist). Many of us wouldn't mind finding out that we aren't really "at fault" for the things that happened in our lives. And more often than you might think, there are important narratives and traumatic experiences to talk about.

I'm not suggesting that we forget the past and focus on the present. I'm simply reminding us to be careful about how we frame narratives in the context of a child's addiction.

As an antidote to psychodynamic biases, we can remind ourselves about the power of genetics. We have no problems saying

---

2. M. Yeh et al., "Parental Beliefs about the Causes of Child Problems: Exploring Racial/Ethnic Patterns," *Journal of the American Academy of Child & Adolescent Psychiatry* 43, no. 5 (2004): 605–12.

that a particular breed of dog has a certain kind of personality, and there is some truth in this. When it comes to people, though, it's as if everyone is born *tabula rasa*—as a blank slate—and that the life story is all that matters. Focusing too much on genetics might seem inhuman, and yet this factor is a reality in addiction and mental health.

Adoption is a case in point. I have worked with adopted children across the spectrum and at various points in their lives—including those newly removed from their first homes and those who are in foster care. I have deep admiration for the resilience of those young people, just as I have for the courage and compassion of the adoptive parents. I say *courage* because they are opening up their hearts and homes to a child in need that genetically may have little in common with them.

Three questions quickly surface whenever I work with adopted children who grow up to develop an addiction:

- Was there some kind of parent-child mismatch or other problem due to the adoption? As in, were the personalities and habits of the adoptive parents and children incompatible for whatever reason?
- Did something traumatic happen to the child prior to the adoption?
- Does the child have identity issues related to being adopted?

Answering all three is essential, but we again need balance.

On the whole, adopted children have no more mental health problems than nonadopted children. It's true that some adopted children have endured horrific trauma. But I also know many children who are adopted at birth, grow up in beautiful homes, are parented well, are generally well behaved, and still become addicted because of their genetic load for the disease. These children are often raised with diligence. But like many other kids who experiment with substances, adopted kids can react to them in a way that triggers a predisposition for addiction. Chasing psychodynamic explanations can hurt these kids more than help them, and adoptive parents are sometimes unfairly blamed.

It's not just parents, by the way, who dig up the past. Young people in treatment can have a tremendous need to write their narrative in a linear manner as well.

Let's say a young person's narrative includes a history of being bullied mercilessly at school and a father who was too demanding. These accounts can be true, and this child will need validation and support in therapy to work through these issues. Sometimes, though, a narrative has a dual purpose. One is to satisfy a child's need for people and events to play a static role. In particular, unsupportive parents become the "bad guys" in the story. The narrative functions to maintain the status quo because the kid sees the journey to recovery as too arduous. In these cases, resentments are never fully surrendered, traumas never overcome.

I sometimes see this dynamic play out in kids who come out as gay or lesbian. Initially, some parents struggle to accept it. Later they come around and offer support. Many young people in this situation are relieved, but others cannot accept the supportive response and actually regress in treatment. Some of these kids need the parents to be the villains in their story. Their narratives downplay their own personal role in addiction and reduce their impetus to change.

This situation is analogous to what happens when people work for a cruel boss. This person's employees can say that any underperformance on their part is a direct result of low morale. Through the "boss is cruel" narrative, employees gain a reason to be late to the office and provide poor customer service. Now imagine that the boss goes to a workshop about leadership. She has a huge revelation about herself and decides to change her tactics. As a result, she works hard to become a kinder, gentler, and more understanding supervisor.

If you're ever involved in such a situation, notice how people respond. Some of your previously disgruntled co-workers will take refuge in the boss's new style. But look to see whether others continue their poor performance. You could make a case that the boss burned all her bridges and that there is no way to salvage morale. You have to wonder, however, if the unresponsive workers have issues of their own and need the boss to act as the villain. Both possibilities beg further exploration.

Bottom line: *Searching through past events in your child's life as a way to understand addiction is tricky. When we rely too heavily on this method, kids can slip through treatment without changing, and parents can get thrown under the bus.*

Chapter 35

Trauma Can Become a Trump Card

Thus far, I have been treading tenderly around the issue of trauma. It is a big one, and it brings up strong emotions like no other. There are few things more invalidating than having your traumatic stories questioned. And yet the topic of trauma, specifically in the context of addiction, can be another double-edged sword.

Let me be clear: I am a firm believer in how traumatic experiences shape us. Trauma in its worst form is called post-traumatic stress disorder (PTSD). People with PTSD can "relive" their trauma in nightmares and flashbacks. They might try to avoid the traumatic memories by isolating themselves or showing little emotion. They might become "aroused" by the event through anxiety, or poor sleep, or anger, or by being startled easily. In short, they are chronically tortured by their psychological wounds and live in a state of recurring high-intensity stress long after the trauma itself.

My experience with PTSD is in working with combat survivors. They range from World War II veterans to veterans of the Iraq wars. These experiences have taught me that trauma is real. The impact it has on people sometimes never goes away. Trauma needs to be treated and understood. For the purposes of this discussion, however, I am going to talk about trauma in general, since many people have endured traumas without having full-on PTSD—or have had PTSD but are now dealing with it partially.

People who experience traumas can be more susceptible to addiction. And people with addiction can be more susceptible to experiencing trauma because of the high-risk lifestyle that often comes with drug use.

Many young persons with addiction experienced trauma before they began to use chemicals. Many others experience trauma after the addiction begins. Fights, sexual assault, abuse (sexual, physical, and emotional), bullying, accidents, overdoses, witnessing deaths or violence, family conflicts, and heated run-ins with the law are just a few examples of what can cause trauma.

We need to be very careful when we help young people with trauma. We need to withhold judgment when people have the courage to be vulnerable enough to share their stories with us. Propriety is everything. That means doing the right thing with the right timing. Dealing with trauma is like eating a hot bowl of soup: You can't go down to the bottom right away because you'll get burned. Some traumatic experiences are so scarring or so acutely hurtful that we need to give the person space for healing—even if we think we know the "solution."

What I have to say below is largely not intended for people who are acutely affected by trauma or otherwise unstable clinically. If this is the case with your child, stick to the "hot soup" approach and trust your child's clinicians.

With this in mind, however, I still notice that people experience trauma differently. Three people can be in a horrific accident or go into combat together, and all three can have different ways of internalizing the experience. I'm not sure why, exactly.

Overall, the topic of trauma is a keystone when it comes to the power of linear narratives. Let's say that someone was seriously traumatized as a child, and he carries the baggage of that trauma. Maybe he has had legitimate PTSD issues. And maybe some of this came at the hand of his parents, who were using at one time but are currently sober. Now, it's been years since the trauma happened, and the kid has had therapy for it. Of course, this doesn't erase what happened, but he is no longer as symptomatic.

At the same time, there's a history of alcoholism in the family, and the kid has been diagnosed with ADHD. So he's loaded with risk factors for addiction, regardless of the trauma. But the way that child has woven his story—perhaps with the help of well-intentioned therapists—is that his family did this to him, and that he used drugs because of the trauma. This story has been written in a rigid way, or inadvertently reinforced, or both. There are resentments that come up in treatment, and these are hard for the child to resolve.

This child's story line gives him a false sense of power. Even if his parents are now in recovery and are trying to make amends, he can still always play that trump card when he feels stressed: *You hit me when I was a little kid*. This becomes a barrier for the child to accept his role in his addiction.

I have a lot of kids who come in with trauma stories and don't want to surrender them. If the trauma symptoms are present, I don't push. I validate and show compassion until they feel heard. Down the road, though, they need to understand that their story, if not framed properly, becomes an insurance against recovery. A mental health issue becomes a crutch, a badge of honor, and a disability in light of the fact that it once gave them hope and an explanation.

If a person is traumatized, is that the only reason he or she uses drugs? Well, sometimes yes, but sometimes no. Sometimes there are other things, like genetic predisposition, or other mental health issues, or behavior problems, or a negative peer group.

Bottom line: *There are many kids who lower the bar in terms of expectations for themselves—or have the bar lowered by others—because they've gone through certain trauma. They need treatment and support, and we have to make sure that the trauma therapy does not diminish their attitude toward change in treatment.*

Chapter 36

When Admissions Are Too Much to Take

Let's say that you and I are working in a large company's mailroom. Our boss assigns us to work in a back room where there are special boxes that need special stamps. Now, these aren't ordinary mail packages. The process for correctly stamping and preparing these boxes is complicated, requiring some higher-level math and a number of calculations.

Well, our boss feels that we are qualified to do the job. So we sit down with an instruction manual and do our best to stamp our first box. Our boss walks in to inspect it, only to tell us that we've done it incorrectly. We are a bit embarrassed, but it's only our first box. So, with a shrug, we try to do better on the next one.

Now imagine a different scenario. Let's assume that nobody walks in the first time we stamp our box incorrectly. We then proceed for the next five years to stamp 100,000 boxes—all incorrectly. No one tells us that we're doing anything wrong. Then one day a supervisor suddenly walks in and says, "Hey, I think you're doing that all wrong."

Think about how much more defensive we'll feel after stamping 100,000 boxes than after stamping one box. The logic behind the feeling is essentially similar in both cases. But after five full years of incorrect stamping, we'll find ourselves becoming irritated and argumentative. We might also invent scenarios and story lines—including some that are implausible—to justify our box-stamping habits.

Why can't we just admit our mistake, even after 100,000 boxes? Because the stakes are much higher. A flood of revelations could follow. We might have to admit that we've potentially stamped *all* the boxes incorrectly, ever since the day we started. We might imagine the catastrophes we created by losing many important packages. We might question the impact of all those lost packages, many with real importance in people's lives. And we might question why we were so self-confident that we didn't double-check the instructions.

The point is that, after five years, we had a false narrative about what we were doing: *We're doing a great job. There are no problems. We are responsible workers.* If we make an admission of error, our narratives are forever suspect. That is bound to cause agony.

And so it is with recovery from addiction.

Through the course of addiction treatment, people come to accept a different perspective on their life story. They finally come to admit they have a problem with using. They own up to the overwhelming evidence that they lost control of their use. They may have to absorb the hurt and suffering they caused other people. One seemingly independent admission starts a chain reaction; one tumbler falls into place, then hundreds of others follow suit, each with an echoing thud that reminds the addict of her hubris and delusion.

Kids may enter substance abuse treatment without any regard for how they have affected others. They may give lip service to the contrary, but the fog of addiction challenges such clarity. Or, they might acknowledge but have little idea of the impact of their actions. And, kids may counter with powerful narratives about how they were wronged by family members or friends.

A young person with addiction will use a narrative to justify her use: *My father never paid attention to me. My mother enabled me too much. I had to take care of my family while they were ill.* Some of these narratives are true, and deserve the utmost in compassion in response (stories of trauma, for example). Some of these narratives are inaccurate only in terms of weight and proportion. That is, they are legitimate but hardly the only cause of addiction, and certainly not a satisfactory justification for kids' behaviors. In their eyes, their life story has to include "villains" or situations out of their control that plummeted them to using uncontrollably, or both.

As they enter therapy, regardless of the type, kids can start to see things differently. Their gradual acceptance of addiction forces a reckoning with past events and relationships.

For example, let's say a young man vilifies his parents during his treatment for addiction, citing a number of valid, but potentially overblown, pieces of evidence. A fight with his father may have turned physical. His mother may have violated his privacy. Maybe his father pushed him too hard into sports. Maybe his parents were too critical of his academic performance or choices in dating. Or, perhaps his parents were unavailable at crucial and difficult points during his childhood.

This young man, in the midst of his recovery, finds a new perspective—one where his parents aren't the antagonists he imagined, at least in magnitude. Suddenly his sense of accountability is greater because there isn't anyone to blame. He then has to reconcile himself with the explosive moments when he, under the influence, lashed out at his loved ones. At that time he was fuming with self-righteousness, but now he is saddled with shame and regret and awkwardness.

Once kids come to accept their addiction, their parents want treatment to start moving quickly. I understand this, but we need to remember that *people can handle only so much change and admission at one time*. The story about stamping boxes doesn't suggest the only reason for their resistance to telling the truth, but I'm framing it in this way to garner a bit of sympathy. There is a reason that kids resist change even while acknowledging the need for it. When I'm in session with young people who are new to recovery, I make it a point to give them some space. That's why people in Alcoholics Anonymous say "Progress, not perfection."

Being sympathetic and patient for change is a two-way street. I've seen clients who've gotten sober after years of turmoil. They are doing quite well, but they tell me in their sessions that their spouses are needling them at every turn. They come into my office and say things such as *He won't cut me any slack!* or *Shouldn't she be happy for me?*

What they don't realize is that, although they have finally found their sobriety and subsequent peace of mind, their spouses still have years of hurt and resentments to process. They have held it in for so long, afraid that an honest expression of emotions would capsize an already fragile vessel. There might have been affairs or abuse or other indiscretions, some more a matter of impaired judgment while using, but deeply hurtful nonetheless. Now that their addicted loved one is sober, they feel emboldened about their own needs and journeys. That takes time.

A recently sober client may have been expecting a warm welcome and a new beginning. The reality is that she might have to "take it" until forgiveness comes or do what she can to help the process. The good news is that time often does come. Many couples proceed together once sufficient resentments and other "bad energies" have been dealt with.

Applied to your family, this might mean that you or someone else may legitimately have issues to work out due to your child's addiction. Your child may be surprised that his return to good graces with loved ones takes a bit longer than he expects. Again, sympathize and extend your newfound wisdom and understanding.

Bottom line: *We must hold firm to the need for kids to change—and, at the same time, recognize how hard it is for young people to accept all the sacrifices that come with change. It can take an enormous amount of courage for people to reconcile with their past.*

Chapter 37

The Difference between Personality and Character

Let's be honest: We all want to believe the best about our children. During the course of addiction, however, everything changes. With all the lying and stealing, all the anger, and all the hostility, we sometimes look across the room at a child who is unfamiliar to us: *Who is this callous and selfish person? How could she do this to us? He doesn't even act like he cares!* In these moments, it isn't uncommon for parents to wonder about their child's very character.

I have had many parents openly question whether their child was sociopathic or beyond hope. This statement may initially strike you as unconscionable, especially if you haven't experienced addiction firsthand. Yet, these are not inappropriate questions, nor are the parents out of bounds for pondering such thoughts. Parents are often told that their child's behavior simply results from the "disease of addiction." But, to be truthful, I think many parents find that to be a bit of a stretch. How could *every* action be the result of addiction? Isn't it possible that my child is just a jerk?

Furthermore, some parents had legitimate concerns about their children's behaviors or tendency to manipulate even *before* they started to use drugs. Those kids weren't "addicts" then.

There is an elephant in the room whenever mental health and addiction issues surface. The elephant is personality, and there are many reasons why such an important topic is rarely discussed head-on. But, of course, we are going to take it head-on right now.

Personality can be defined in many ways. For the purposes of this discussion, let's define *personality* as "a collection of patterns that govern our responses to situations, whether they are emotional, behavioral, or intellectual." Put more simply, a person's personality determines how they

- see the world
- visualize relationships
- react to stress
- regulate their moods
- respond to feedback from others
- trust other people

Personality is formed through an interplay of life experiences, environmental exposures, and genetics.

Before moving on, let's separate the word *character* from the word *personality*. Personality is a collection of traits, observations made about a person's patterns removed from judgment. Due to symbolism and attribution, on the other hand, *character* can be a loaded word. Character refers to observations plus moral judgment.

The word *character* has many implications. There is something labeling and restrictive about it. When we say Vincent has a history of stealing, we are making an observation. We might then inquire about how Vincent interacts with people and perceives his world. But when we say Vincent is a "bad kid" because of his stealing, we are making a character judgment.

It is important that we not introduce morally laden terms in addiction, lest we return to the stereotype of addiction as a moral defect. However, we need to talk about personality as patterns that influence the course of an individual's addiction.

When we discuss personality in addiction, the focus is much more objective. Some young people are more thrill seeking than others. Some are willing to take on more risk. Some fail to see the consequences of their actions right away. Some are more stubborn. Some are better at justifying their behaviors through intellect. Some do well with feedback, while others feel persecuted easily. Some are willing to go with the flow, and others are rigid or controlling. We don't say they are good or bad kids based on these traits; we simply acknowledge that these traits exist.

I'm sure you can already tell why personality is rarely discussed openly in mental health circles.

Bottom line: *Talking about a child's personality requires honest appraisal removed from moral sentiments.*

Chapter 38

Let's Talk about Personality

The topic of personality is a heavily researched one in psychiatric literature. The degree to which it is forthrightly discussed in clinical practice pales in comparison.

The concept of personality is usually not fully entertained by doctors and therapists until a kid's behavior reaches a pathological state. Then it is referred to as a *personality disorder*. Until personality goes to an extreme, clinicians stay away from necessary conversations about a child's emerging temperament. They're afraid that the mere mention of personality will label and stigmatize a child in need. Their sentiment comes from the right place, but the lack of discussion does a great disservice.

In reality, personality often starts to emerge in kids at an early age. You've probably seen traits in your own child that were present from the time she was two or three years old that are still present today. The kid who's scared to leave home for the first day of kindergarten can be the same one who's scared to leave for the first day of college.

When I was in my child psychiatry fellowship, we were clearly discouraged from talking about personality. The contention was that children do not have stable personalities until adulthood. Until then, their personalities can change significantly. I agree. The idea of labeling a ten-year-old with a personality disorder is offensive and ridiculous.

However, if we would talk about personality without going to such extremes, we'd make therapeutic work so much more tangible and transparent to everyone involved. We could say that a child has a few personality traits that need to be noted, even though they don't add up to a disorder. We could say Jasmine has a tendency to tell tall tales without implying that she is going to grow up to be a sociopath, or that she will behave this way forever.

Kids who have a hard time seeing things from the perspective of others may have an even harder time when their mood is low. But if the trait persists even when their mood is fine, this suggests that personality is part of the story.

By talking more openly about personality, we could also stop pretending that diagnoses such as depression, anxiety, trauma, and even addiction magically explain all of the behaviors of addicted kids. Instead of ramming a square peg into a round hole, clinically speaking, we could call it what it is.

Depression can be there, for sure, and trauma can definitely be added to the fire. But maybe one child is still more opportunistic than others or has a harder time walking in someone else's shoes. This is not a prediction about his future. It is simply a description of who he has been up until now, based upon his patterns of behavior and interactions with others.

Furthermore, plenty of evidence suggests that personality matters in addiction. It is a little discussed but well-known fact that people with personality disorders have higher rates of addiction. This goes for narcissistic personality disorder, antisocial personality disorder, and borderline personality disorder, to name a few diagnoses. People with these personality disorders are sometimes believed to have a worse prognosis in treatment. So when it comes to extremes, at least, we know that personalities influence addiction.

Let's discuss conduct disorder in more detail. This diagnosis is given to children and adolescents whose behaviors consistently demonstrate a lack of regard for societal rules and the feelings of other people. When we talk about mental health disorders that co-occur with addiction, conduct disorder is actually the most common—much more than depression, anxiety, or ADHD. This might surprise you, but it is the truth.

Some kids with conduct disorder will go on to develop antisocial personality, which is also defined by a tendency to be insensitive to societal norms and the rights and feelings of others. In addition, conduct disorder can bode a worse prognosis for addiction treatment. Kids with conduct disorder are more likely to have legal issues and more likely to have mental health diagnoses in the long run. Those who develop disruptive behaviors early in life along the lines of conduct disorder may also use drugs earlier than other kids.

If you break down conduct disorder into the language of personality, you will talk about kids who can be more callous or unemotional compared to others, more thrill seeking, or more willing to obtain end goals with less regard for the means to those ends. Once again, personality matters.

Let's put this all together by reminding ourselves to look for two elements in any diagnosis—the disease process and personal factors. Again, taking hypertension as an example, there is the disease process of increased blood pressure and all the variables that play a role in this symptom. Then there are the personal factors that contribute to the high blood pressure—lack of exercise, a family history of heart disease, and the like.

If we look at any mental health diagnosis the same way, we can see a similar pair of factors. There is, for example, the disease process of pathologic anxiety. This includes all the heightened reactions in the brain and the body's response to the anxiety. There are also personal factors that govern anxiety. People with this diagnosis may

- be very sensitive to emotional feedback or stress
- feel judged by others rather quickly

- be shy and isolative by nature, leaving them imprisoned by their limited perspectives
- have a strong family history of anxiety

In addition, there may have been incidents in their lives that shaped their anxious reactions.

Just as a person's eating habits and exercise habits play a role in their high blood pressure, a child's developing personality is important to mental health problems they might encounter with or without addiction. Not dealing with personality in treatment is like treating people with high blood pressure and not asking them to change their lifestyle.

Bottom line: *In psychiatry, we tend to talk about personality only in terms of disorder. Instead, we could talk about personality traits that fall between the extremes, making for a richer and more useful conversation about our kids.*

Chapter 39

Balancing "Nature" and "Nurture" in Personality

When parents start to talk about their child's personality, they suddenly become interested in how it came to be: *Dave is just like his father, and his father was an alcoholic.* The standard answer from psychologists is that personality results from a combination of nature (genetics) and nurture (life experiences).

Why is a discussion about nature versus nurture so important? Because of our need for attribution. If they forget to make this distinction, parents will find it hard to look at their child's emerging personality in an objective way.

When it comes to physical features like hair color or height, we don't question genetics. When we talk about breeds of animals and the kinds of temperaments they display, we accept the role of genetics. But when it comes to our personalities and anything that cannot be assessed with our five physical senses, suddenly genetics are hard to talk about.

On the whole, I believe genetics are undervalued in the discussion about nature versus nurture. This might be due to the egalitarian appeal of nurture—the idea that skilled parenting and other favorable life circumstances from the start mean we can grow up to be anything and do anything.

The concept that genetics influence personality traits has the opposite effect. It makes us feel like robots from a factory. We see ourselves as predetermined and programmed to follow fixed routines—machines who live out their existence without a hint of free will.

I am certainly not suggesting that our genetic code dooms us and our children to a certain fate. However, the "personality is only about nurture" concept leads to needlessly painful discussions for parents. If genetics aren't a major player in the personality game, then the attribution starts to flow in the direction of the home environment and parenting styles. All the fingers start pointing at the parents. They can end up filled with regret and saying that we "woulda, coulda, shoulda" done things differently.

Now, there's no doubt that kids' environments and experiences significantly shape their personality. Children are affected by their family situations, experiences with friends, and traumas. But then again, a child's genetic loading can be strong enough to overpower nurturing. If someone has a strong family history of addiction, for example, then there's a possibility he can become addicted even if he's adopted by a new family and grows up in a different country.

Most parents have witnessed firsthand the impact of genetics on personality. They often see it when their children are at an early age—during the toddler years or even earlier. Many traits are set forth before any major life event steers it: a child's sense of humor, penchant for anger, ability to transition between activities, athletic ability, and more. Not surprisingly, some of these traits are preserved over time.

Knowing about this provides useful information for clinical care down the road. For example, consider a child before the age of five who feels abnormal anxiety about separating from parents. This kid might refuse to start school and have difficulty with learning new activities. So if she complains of anxiety in the midst of addiction, it's not a surprise. I know, based on developmental history, that her personality was marked by higher levels of self-doubt, rigidity, or both, even prior to drug use. In turn, this gives me additional confidence in exploring the symptoms as true anxiety rather than dismissing them as by-products of craving and withdrawal.

A good way to think about personality is to say that a Chevy will always remain in some fundamental ways a Chevy. We can make it a great Chevy. We can replace the engine, the tires, and the seats. We can also install a new sound system. But fundamentally, the car is still a Chevy and not a Toyota, nor a Ford. Likewise, some personality traits are hardwired and act like parameters. Our experiences and environment greatly affect who we become—but within those genetic parameters. Personality is a relatively *static* quality, meaning that it takes a longer time to change than *dynamic* qualities (such as feeling sad).

It is important to note, however, that personalities *can* change. Imagine every person as a musical instrument that is capable of playing a range of notes. Some of those notes are melodic and some are harsh. Addiction can highlight the harsh notes, but this does not mean the instrument is beyond repair. I believe that the melody is still there and simply isn't being expressed.

So take heart if you have been concerned about your child's emerging temperament. I have seen many young men with a long history of violence and intense addiction go through dramatic change. Sometimes it's about maturity. Sometimes it's a spiritual awakening. And sometimes the transformations are forged through positive relationships.

Bottom line: *It is important to balance our bias toward "nurture" with a conversation about "nature." That way, we can avoid unnecessary attribution.*

Chapter 40

The Difference between Guilt and Shame

There is a rat in a cage in a white room like the ones used in lab experiments. The cage has clear plastic walls and is built like a maze. The rat is proficient at getting around in the maze. In one corner of the cage, it can eat food. In another, there is a potential mate. In yet another, there is a wheel for the rat to run on.

Now, let's assume that in another part of the cage, there are some baby rats. In response, the rat does what it is genetically programmed to do: It runs on the wheel, cares for its young, mates, and eats food.

Eventually the scientist at this lab introduces a drug to the rat. The animal has to tap a button to dispense this drug. This chemical is addictive, and the rat succumbs to its pull. The rat suspends all activities to keep getting the drug. Its young are neglected. The wheel sits still. The rat's mate is ignored. The food is not consumed. The only significant activity for this rat is getting more of the drug.

Is this rat morally corrupt? Does this rat ignore its young because of a weakness in its character or moral fiber? Of course not. That would be a ridiculous notion. The rat does what it does because its brain places the highest priority on the obtaining of the drug. The drug matters above all else, and it will be attained at any cost. There is no question of morality. It is a matter of neurochemical rewards gone awry.

So it is with addiction in people. Many parents feel personally hurt by their addicted child's "immoral" behaviors. And, in retrospect, the kids themselves feel a deep shame about their deeds. When they enter treatment, they cannot reconcile their values with what they have done to others as a result of their use.

Yet, in some fundamental way, these kids are like the rat. They do not steal from their parents and use violent means to get what they want solely because of moral bankruptcy. They do not betray their friends and manipulate others because they lack ethical fortitude. They do so because their brain's circuitry demands that they seek a reward, no matter what the cost. For someone who is addicted, the ends do justify the means.

I can't tell you the number of times young people have sat in my office with the unbearable weight of regret. Their past behaviors make them question who they are on a fundamental level: *Why did I cheat on my boyfriend? Why did I pawn my family heirlooms? How could anyone do this to another person?* The shame becomes an immense obstacle in recovery.

This is when I offer the rat analogy. But I don't do this to absolve kids of accountability. I simply want to help them understand that, in neurochemical terms, the deck is stacked against them when they are using drugs. Most of them would have never done what they did unless they were in a vicious cycle of craving.

This usually assuages kids but rarely reassures them all the way, which indicates that they still have a conscience. The conversation also rekindles hope and suggests that kids should avoid stacking the deck against themselves in the future.

Some parents might want a child with addiction to feel shame. Perhaps they think that shame will be of some therapeutic value in the long run. If young people do something wrong, they should, of course, feel remorse about it. When I encounter shame in treatment settings, however, it is almost always a detriment to progress.

Here's why. First, let's distinguish shame from guilt. Guilt is a feeling of culpability (in an emotional sense) but does not necessarily invoke personal wrongdoing (as it does in the legal sense). Children can feel guilty about their parents' divorce and still know they aren't responsible for the divorce. Likewise, kids can feel guilty about the death of a friend who was using drugs, believing that they could have done something to prevent the death. Again, these kids don't necessarily feel responsible, but they have plenty of personal regret.

Shame, on the other hand, is an emotion that frequently arises when someone feels responsible. When it comes to shame, there is little doubt about who is accountable. Shame implicates a person directly: *Yeah, it was me*. Shame makes that person feel everyone's eyes on him or her. It is a scarlet letter.

In my experience, shame usually goes down in one of two ways. First, shameful addicts flog themselves. They isolate, engage in self-deprecating talk, feel suicidal, cut themselves, or take on more responsibility than they should. This self-punitive approach may be seen as appropriate.

But, like most stimuli, the impact of self-punishment wears off over time, no matter how powerfully or profoundly it initially occurs. When addicts feel they have "done their time" or "paid their dues," it's back to using.

Second, shame can make kids give up. They figure that since they are already worthless and beyond redemption, they might as well use again. Worse yet, they might resort to suicide.

Either way, shame is generally unproductive in treatment.

This does not rule out any room for morality in addiction. Morally reprehensible acts *are* done by people on a daily basis while under the influence of drugs, while in withdrawal, or while in severe craving. And it is true that some people with addiction acted in questionable ways even prior to drug use. When the focus is on accountability rather than on shame or guilt, it allows everyone involved to move forward instead of wallow in the past, and it lays a solid foundation for recovery.

Bottom line: *Our kids can be held accountable for their behaviors in the midst of drug use. At the same time, they can live without internalizing a moralistic brand of shame on their very person—one that will permanently rob them of hope and eventually derail them from recovery.*

Chapter 41

Emotional Hyperalgesia: When Depression Isn't Depression and Anxiety Isn't Anxiety

Have you ever sat in a hot tub for a while and then jumped into a swimming pool? How did the water feel? Freezing, obviously. But is it really that cold? Of course not. After a while, your body recalibrates to the pool. Your body adjusts to the change in temperature. No big deal.

Now assume you are passed out in the hot tub and someone suddenly throws you into the pool. Having forgotten that you were in the hot tub in the first place, chances are that you might have a stronger reaction to the change in temperature.

Well, this is similar to what happens when your child initially becomes sober. Kids want to change, but the experience is sobering in more ways than one. Loose stools, headaches, chills, tremors, seizures, nightmares, insomnia—these are just a few of the symptoms they might have to endure. Some substances cause worse withdrawal symptoms than others. And the physical symptoms are sometimes the least tricky to manage.

The hot tub analogy is important in many ways. For one thing, we can use it as a reminder to sympathize with our children's struggles in the first stages of recovery. Trust me, it isn't easy. The fact that so many go through with it is a testament to the courage of young people who finally decide to put aside short-term gains for the sake of long-term hope. In addition, the analogy can give context to many of the complaints that emerge when children first come into treatment.

Often during recovery—especially the first month—kids make some physical and psychological complaints: *My back is killing me; I think it's the bed. I'm trying my best, but I just can't pay attention. I am so anxious that I feel like I am crawling out of my skin; I just need something to help.* Some of these complaints are completely legitimate. Others are legitimate but also signal that the kids are recalibrating to an unfamiliar reality; those symptoms will get better in time. When kids feel unhappy, nervous, or irritable, our job as clinicians and parents is to give them reassurance. We focus on treating the symptoms that won't just go away when they get used to the temperature of the water.

Another way to look at this is to explore the concept of hyperalgesia. *Hyperalgesia* means increased sensitivity to pain. This is something that happens to people who are on pain medications for a long time, even if they are not addicted and take them as prescribed. Remember that our brains and bodies have a beautiful economy that works on supply and demand. When people's brains are swimming in opiates, they recalibrate their natural threshold for pain. Once they no longer have access to medication, they find certain conditions to be more painful than the rest of us would.

The same thing happens in addiction—quite literally, in fact, when kids are using heroin or pain medications. But more important, an *emotional hyperalgesia* also takes hold. This means their threshold for pain—not just for tolerating pain but for difficult emotions—goes way down. They feel stressed by the daily treatment schedule. They cannot tolerate much frustration. Any setback is bound to make them feel anger, dejection, or panic.

Emotional hyperalgesia makes it confusing for any newly sober person to know whether their anxiety results from craving, from not wanting to be in treatment, or from a true anxiety disorder. They're not sure whether their sadness results simply from coming to terms with reality or from real depression—or whether the anger they feel is pent-up resentment against their parents or just an adjustment to such drastic change. Young people's emotions may be real, but their sense of proportion and magnitude can get lost.

One time my wife went shopping for a perfume, and I went to the store with her to be an extra nose. There were so many fragrances. The salesperson offered us coffee beans to sniff between fragrance samples, which supposedly cleansed the smelling palate, if you will, allowing us to distinguish one fragrance from another. After taking a few whiffs of fragrances like *chateau d'odeur* and *redolence du fromage*, I just couldn't tell the difference between them. And after leaving the store, the memory of the smells stayed with me for a few hours.

So it is with addiction. The disease so overwhelms children's brains that, from an emotional standpoint, they start to lose their taste for subtleties. Their emotions are all over the place. Many addicts cannot initially tell the difference between intensity and intimacy, the former being a matter of strength and frequency, and the latter being a true closeness. They cannot tell the difference between honest, supportive feedback and outright rejection. They hang out with peers who accept them and like them, but who aren't good for them. When people they love reach out to them, the kids only see conflicts. They fall head over heels in romantic relationships and go too fast in possibly dangerous friendships. Patience is required by all parties to help these kids adjust and relearn what they knew in more hopeful times.

I see many parents desperately advocating for their children in treatment when they hear these emotional pleas from them. There is nothing wrong with this. On the contrary, there is beauty in it. I realize every day that parents' love for their children is unconditional (despite our knowledge that their children's love for them is conditional, indeed). However, it is the norm and not the exception that young people will have a litany of complaints when they enter any kind of treatment and face the realities of sobriety.

Sometimes parents defend such complaints to the treatment staff, not understanding the process of recovery or the dynamics of emotional hyperalgesia. They feel that some symptom is being undertreated. They wonder if their children are right to be disproportionately angry about treatment. Their children are well aware of the parents' change in tune. Suddenly, these children see a break in the perimeter, so to speak, and their complaints crescendo as other complaints are thrown in as well. The parents angrily side with their children, and the treatment contract with the staff is eventually broken. Parents come to realize only after the fact that their kids were simply reverting to their addicted ways, doing whatever it took to return to the status quo—the hot tub.

Bottom line: *Align with the treatment team as much as possible. Not all clinics are the same, and many complaints about treatment are legitimate. Even so, act on a foundation of emotional objectivity and leadership. Remember to advocate for your child in a way that does not break therapeutic bonds.*

Chapter 42

Looks Like "Whac-A-Mole" to Me—Conservation of Energy in Addiction

Think about the ecosystem—the food chain, specifically. Animals eat plants. These animals, in turn, are eaten by other animals. When these animals die, they are decomposed by microbes and bugs that nourish other creatures, which are then eaten by other animals.

Whether we're talking about the food chain or the process of recycling, the general idea is the same. As the laws of thermodynamics tell us, energy cannot be created or destroyed. It can only be changed from one form to another.

I find parallels to this law when it comes to treatment for addiction. Addicts have a kind of "energy," if you will. I don't mean karma, and I'm not using the word in any New Age sense. Addicts simply have a psychological intensity that other people lack. When people in treatment become sober, their addictive energy doesn't disappear. That's why there is no quick cure. What happens is that they take that self-destructive energy, chop it up into more digestible pieces, and find more productive venues for it. In the end, they have to find something that will fill the same void that addiction tried to fill.

In psychology, one term for this process is called *sublimation*. For example, a person who struggles with aggression becomes a boxer in order to channel the anger more appropriately. Many people in recovery operate on a similar principle. They take up other interests. They attend Twelve Step meetings. They form new relationships. They talk about their addiction. They volunteer and help others who struggle. I've seen people in recovery take up gardening, become professors, and even set up their own treatment centers.

The conservation of energy does not apply well to disorders such as schizophrenia, dementia, or traumatic brain injury. But in many other circumstances, conservation of energy can be a helpful way to think about your addicted child.

Anxiety comes to mind as a perfect example. Because of the many faces of anxiety, parents often do not recognize when it is a problem. Consider a girl who as a toddler was clingy with her mother. Several years later, this child struggles with separation anxiety. She refuses to attend school in first grade due to emotional distress. In fifth grade, she starts to "milk" sick days as a means to come home. In the seventh grade, she has to come home from summer camp. She then develops social anxiety and does whatever she can to fit in.

In high school, this girl avoids tougher classes. She tries hard to control her environment, possibly as a way to minimize any risk. She is also self-conscious about her image and appearance.

By the time she enters college, she has learned to cope with her anxiety but not necessarily in a healthy way. She is still controlling and rigid. On the surface, she isn't anxious, as she was earlier. In fact, she is articulate and seemingly composed. But this is only because she has managed her environment to avoid any surprise or great challenge.

When this young woman becomes addicted, things start to unravel. She tries to control her use and then her eating. She finally agrees to enter treatment but has panic attacks. She says she wants to become sober but will not leave her boyfriend, who still uses.

Anxiety in this case changes from one form to another over the course of a life. At times, it may not even appear like anxiety at all. Using the conservation of energy theory, this young woman's anxiety did not vanish. It just changed from worrying and clinging to control and rigidity.

Keep in mind that anxiety—just like sadness or anger—is not a bad thing in and of itself. Sometimes, in fact, anxiety can be quite useful. It is, after all, just a feeling. When I use the word *anxiety* in this chapter, I am referring to pathologic anxiety that is disproportionate to any cause and impairs a person's ability to function in daily life over a sustained period of time.

Consider another example, this time a boy who gets very angry. His parents send him to treatment for drug use and for anger issues. In the process of getting to know this young man, I discover that he is actually anxious. He gets angry when he feels he is backed into a corner, and that tends to happen for him a lot. Anger is the only way he knows how to get people off his back.

Again, we need to remember that many psychological energies are re-formed and not destroyed. Then we can identify kids who need treatment even when they say they have no problems.

Do you remember the old arcade game called Whac-A-Mole? It's the one where you get a mallet, and the objective is to hit moles that pop up at random from various holes. Well, sometimes kids in treatment remind me of Whac-A-Mole: Their addictive energy changes from one form to another—popping up out of another hole, so to speak. For example, a girl with a controlling nature can go from addiction to cutting herself to having an eating disorder to a destructive relationship to having depression—and back to addiction.

This is related to what people call *cross addictions*. I have seen people get sober temporarily only to pick up some other vice. It could be stealing, playing video games, shopping for hours on end, or developing an eating disorder. Some girls come to treatment and start to binge and purge as soon as they are sober.

The pattern is incredibly telling. That addictive energy has to go somewhere!

Did you know that a higher proportion of girls with eating disorders have co-occurring substance abuse problems compared to the proportion of girls with primary addiction issues who have co-occurring eating disorders? On this two-way street, there is double the traffic from one direction to another. So a typical girl with bulimia is more likely to have a co-occurring substance abuse problem than a typical girl with a substance abuse problem is to have bulimia. This is important, because many addiction clinics recognize co-occurring eating disorders, while many eating disorder facilities do not have adequate treatments or screenings for addiction. Again, there are powerful biases at work here, including parents with resistance to seeing their daughters as addicts. Even the psychological community would rather describe young women as depressed or traumatized than addicted.

As I have warned when discussing the delusions of linear narratives, we don't always have to know exactly how conditions develop over time. It is helpful, however, to trust your clinicians to find some core traits in any self-destructive patterns that consume your child. The important thing to remember is that underneath the Whac-A-Mole game, there is a common mechanism.

Bottom line: *Understand that psychological energy is not destroyed or created. It just shifts in form, which can create a series of challenges in recovery. If your child is willing to enter recovery, think about the kinds of activities (including spiritual) and relationships that might sufficiently take addiction's place.*

Chapter 43

For Whom the Bell Tolls, It Tolls for Those with ADHD

ADHD is a very real and potentially debilitating condition. Research is rather conclusive in pointing out that people with ADHD are more likely to struggle academically, socially, and vocationally. They are even more likely to get into car accidents. In recent years, there has been controversy about the liberty with which the terms *ADHD* and *ADD* (attention deficit disorder) are thrown around. We must also take into account the rampant abuse of ADHD medications by a variety of individuals, from mothers to college students to professionals and athletes. Add the issue of addiction into the mix, and we get one delicate topic for discussion.

It's no wonder that entire books are written about ADHD alone. All kinds of details can be found elsewhere, but I am going to provide you with a big picture. In this chapter, I want to talk about ADHD as a cultural phenomenon and then discuss some caveats for consideration when ADHD and addiction coexist. I will provide a little more clinical information than I do with other diagnoses I mention for this reason: Unlike many other co-occurring mental health issues, the medications used to treat ADHD can be diverted and abused.

Think about a bell curve—the bell-shaped graph that tapers down on the ends. When we look at people in groups, any characteristic they share can be plotted on a graph, and many of those graphs would resemble a bell curve. We could create a curve for weight, for height, or for IQ. All of us will fall on a specific point on each of these curves. People who have uncommon characteristics—such as being very tall or very short—will fall on the two tapered ends. Most people will fall somewhere in the broader middle portions of the curves.

Remember the inefficient locomotion syndrome that we used to describe children who run slowly? (See chapter 28: "Symbolism in Mental Health Treatment.") If we put all children on a bell curve for this syndrome, one end would represent gifted runners, and the other end would represent slower-than-average runners.

Now, suppose we conclude that running too slowly is somehow a determining factor for human misery. In this imaginary culture, perhaps people who run slowly have a difficult time in school, keeping jobs, and establishing relationships. We would next need to choose a point on the bell curve where we want to make that diagnosis. Is it the bottom 5 percent? Is it the bottom 10 percent? Or does the dividing line fall on some other point on the curve? This is a silly example, but it helps us see why a diagnosis such as ADHD can become controversial.

Consider inattention, which is just one core symptom of ADHD. If we plotted all people on a bell curve according to their ability to pay attention, the precious few with "perfect" attention would be on one end; those who have to read this page five times to remember what it says would be on the other end. Most of us would fall somewhere between the two extremes.

Let's expand on this example. There are kids who pay attention well, and those who don't pay attention well. There are children who fidget more than others, kids who are more hyperactive than others, and those who are more distractible. We can place any of these symptom clusters on corresponding curves. We can then choose a certain point on these curves, where we can draw a line through it and say, "Okay, anybody who falls to the left of this line has a problem with ADHD."

This is not a completely arbitrary process, because there are points on the ADHD curve where people experience real distress. I believe even those with skepticism about ADHD will accept that reality. However, the point at which we choose to draw the line is what becomes controversial. This cutoff point seems to move around more than people are willing to openly admit. Some only consider ADHD when the impairment is obvious to everyone around. Others wonder about having ADHD whenever their attention is "less than perfect."

Across the world, 3 to 7 percent or so of children meet criteria for ADHD. This includes less industrialized cultures than ours. However, the people in these cultures—while acknowledging that something is different with these children—might not call it ADHD. Also, daily life for these kids might be structured so that the condition is less of a problem, leading to a lower level of distress. Perhaps those whom we would diagnose with ADHD will grow up to work at a job or play another role in their village where the ability to pay attention doesn't matter so much.

In developed countries, there's an enormous push for success. We want all children to believe that they can become the next president of the United States. We want them to succeed at whatever they do—to walk up to the plate and swing for the fences. In many ways, that's great. I'm certainly not knocking what we do to create a sense of possibility in our kids. However, our beliefs create enormous pressure on them to uniformly meet certain standards. And when they don't, it's hard for us to watch them fail. We tend to think in extremes: Either you succeed or you need help. When a kid falls into a gray area of the bell curve, we're not sure how to deal with that.

One reason why ADHD is overdiagnosed in our country is that the diagnosis might be used more often for children in competitive classrooms, and for those who come from foster care or areas of poverty. Go visit a competitive private school and take note of how many children there have been diagnosed with ADHD. Other variables are certainly involved, but our high expectations are one aspect. Our ongoing themes of symbolism and attribution clearly apply here. The constant pressure to succeed changes our definition of the disease.

I was once at a conference, listening to someone talk about ADHD. Everybody in the room was a physician, and the speaker was a "let's go hard at ADHD" kind of guy, which is fine. He gave us a questionnaire designed to reveal ADHD symptoms. When we finished the survey, he asked people to raise their hands if they thought they had ADHD. Something like 80 percent of the people in that room thought they did. And these are physicians! So it's clear that not even the medical community has a complete grasp of this bell curve and the sliding threshold.

The shifting definition of ADHD illustrates a key issue in mental health treatment. Social norms, patient expectations, academic pressures, and competition are just some of the variables that move the cut-off line. Now let's talk about a problem with ADHD in the context of addiction.

Young people with addiction are impulsive. They make rash judgments. They get carried away in the moment and act without considering the consequences. Young people with ADHD are also sometimes impulsive. So what happens when we treat the impulsivity in a young person with addiction and ADHD? The *impulsivity* related to the addiction would also get treated, resulting in better sobriety rates, right?

Intuitively, this makes sense. Unfortunately, research thus far says that treating ADHD when a child is already addicted to substances does not necessarily help sobriety rates very much. ADHD could be a risk factor for addiction, and treating ADHD early may or may not protect against the development of later addiction (although such treatment will not cause harm or addiction in most cases). Parents who believe in treating the ADHD aggressively while their child is addicted might be surprised to learn that although the ADHD symptoms improve, the rates of sobriety do not necessarily improve with them.

The word *impulsivity* again points out the problems with jargon. A child with ADHD who gets too emotional in the moment, says something he shouldn't, and is immediately embarrassed could be called impulsive. A child who plans to run away from treatment with other kids, and then goes to the gas station down the road to buy cigarettes, and then decides to come back to treatment...well, that is a sequence of events that we cannot completely attribute to ADHD. In general, I find that impulsivity related to addiction requires more planning and forethought, and is not always the same as the impulsiveness we describe in ADHD. This is supported by convincing new research that suggests the neuropathways for impulsivity in ADHD and addiction are not as similar as we think.

Another issue is that people mistake the improvement they see with medication for an actual diagnosis. I see kids who take their sibling's Adderall or other ADHD medication and say, "I can pay attention better when I take it, so I must have ADHD." This is a frequently cited mantra with addicted children, as they will invariably complain about their lack of focus in early sobriety that is sometimes due more to their chronic substance abuse than ADHD alone.

What I tell them is this: "If I give you insulin and your blood sugar goes down, this does not necessarily mean that you have diabetes. If I give you hypertension medication and your blood pressure goes down, this does not necessarily mean that you have hypertension. If I give you an antibiotic, it will kill some germs in your body, but this does not necessarily mean that you have an infection."

The fallacy here is a kind of a "better living through chemistry" argument: Let's just give ourselves a diagnosis and take the drugs that enhance our performance and health. When it comes to addiction and mental health issues in kids, this can be dangerous. The diversion and abuse of ADHD medications is a widespread practice partially reinforced by such thinking.

If you have a child with addiction and ADHD, take comfort in the fact that there are many young people in recovery with ADHD who can take their medications responsibly without signs of abuse or diversion. I treat many of them myself, even with stimulant medications (if they are safe and necessary). The key is to partner closely with treatment providers so you don't get lulled into any of the dilemmas above.

Here are several more caveats for parents who want to navigate the world between ADHD and addiction:

- ADHD and drug use can have combined detrimental effects. For example, cannabis can impair memory. ADHD impairs attention. If people with ADHD smoke too much cannabis, they will have trouble both remembering *and* paying attention.
- No diagnostic procedure for ADHD is foolproof. This goes for neuropsychological computer testing as well. I have seen far too many kids feign symptoms or admit to getting high then taking a "test" for ADHD to secure a subsequent prescription. Get many data points at different stages in sobriety to establish a diagnosis.
- Medication diversion and abuse are a reality. Even if your child does not abuse her medications, she might be offered money or drugs in exchange for them. If at all possible, have a third party (like you) dispense and store the medication. Having routine urine drug screens at a physician's office is a good idea as well, at least early on in sobriety.
- Kids who abuse their medications will commonly take

more than a normal dosage orally, or try to crush and snort the pills. Most young people who abuse ADHD medications are not addicts but are using the drugs for another reason—to cram for tests, for example. That is no excuse for such a risky undertaking. However, the profile of a young person who is likely to abuse ADHD medications, sell them to someone else, or give them away is similar to the profile of a kid in addiction treatment.

- If you choose to treat your child with addiction for ADHD, consider a nonabusable medication like atomoxetine or guanfacine first. If you have to choose a stimulant, ask for one that is harder to abuse and longer acting.
- Remember that the treatment of ADHD sometimes prolongs the detection of addiction. This is because the ADHD medication can make the child much more functional despite his drug use. A young person who smokes too much cannabis, for example, may do better in school in large part because of his ADHD medication. ("My grades are fine; leave me alone.") Without the medication, the young person's addiction may be exposed earlier through his struggles. It is not uncommon for addicted young people to use ADHD medications to stay awake so they can party longer or use more drugs.
- If your child has a history of an eating disorder or body image issues, watch out. As stated earlier, girls in particular (but boys, too) like to use stimulant medications to keep their weight low and suppress the need to eat. So the summary from the addict's perspective might be, "I'm productive, keeping my figure, and can party all night. What's the problem?"
- The social impairment caused by ADHD is often

downplayed in comparison to the academic issues. Some children with ADHD are simply less savvy socially than their peers. This matters in addiction treatment because it will impact their ability to maintain healthy sober relationships.

Bottom line: *ADHD is a real issue for many young people. It can be treated successfully even with addiction. However, when it comes to ADHD and your addicted child, be aware of the societal forces and jargon that can create confusion and bias.*

Chapter 44

Sobriety Is Not a Ticket to Nirvana

There is a long-held notion that if we can just get our children sober, they will return to "normal" and become wholesome. There are circumstances when this is true. More often, however, recovery is not that simple. The young person, especially early in recovery, can continue to struggle despite sobriety. This may be unwanted news, but it is reality. That's because addiction doesn't "just happen" to kids. My experience is that many kids who develop addiction later were actually vulnerable to having a multitude of problems in life, ranging from learning disabilities to psychiatric conditions to behavioral issues. Addiction just happens to be one of the eventual pitfalls for these vulnerable youth, along with a number of other mental health issues.

It is commonly suggested that young people need continued care after they become sober solely because their addiction has stunted their development, implying that when they catch up they are "good to go." There is truth in this. Still, I believe that the concept of a kid with multiple vulnerabilities is a more accurate estimation of why some children are more apt to develop addiction in the first place.

This is a big deal. Among other things, it means that even when kids are sober, they can still wrestle with the underlying vulnerabilities, like a tendency for risk taking, an eating disorder, or an inability to keep relationships.

The situation is similar to what members of Alcoholics Anonymous call the "dry drunk" syndrome. People who have stopped drinking can still have plenty of rough edges in terms of their emotions and behaviors. Some of these people developed addiction in middle age or later, meaning that stunted development is a poor explanation for their continued woes. Being sober gives them a chance to work on those vulnerabilities, and the process takes time.

This is where we need to talk again about the role of risk factors. Think of these as small gasoline spills that no one is noticing. When people do something to trigger one of these vulnerabilities (like using drugs frequently), it's as if they're throwing a match on those spills. The risks are exposed and spark into flames. Putting out the fire through sobriety will help for sure but may not make the original spills go away.

Using another example, there are risk factors that make some people more vulnerable to heart disease. These include smoking, inactivity, and uncontrolled blood pressure. Other factors may put people with heart disease in a worse prognostic category, meaning their chance of having poor treatment outcomes is higher. Improving their cardiac function temporarily through clinical practice does not all of the sudden cause the patient to start exercising or quit smoking. In short, the journey of recovery does not end at sobriety. Recovery will require continued diligence and patience from all parties involved. Taken from a different perspective, do not be disappointed if your newly sober child is not exactly how you envisioned him or her yet.

Next, understanding risk factors is important because many addicted youth have siblings who may or may not be addicted yet. Paying attention to the red flags below might help you prevent repeated headaches in the future.

Just as there are risk factors for physical diseases, there are risk factors for addiction. Currently, most diagnostic measures for addiction only look at the seriousness of current drug use and the impairment that results. Some kids experiment with drugs and never become addicted. Some do. And, our current assessments do not do a great job of figuring out which kids will be at higher risk for developing addiction and which kids will not do as well in treatment. So they don't reliably identify young people at high risk and those with a troubling trajectory. Research is emerging, however, and here are some general findings:

Children who show disruptive behaviors early on or experience early mental health problems are vulnerable for a host of issues later in adolescence. Like I said, one of those is addiction. Some kids have both of these risk factors.

Conduct disorder, as described earlier, is definitely one risk factor for addiction. In addition, kids with conduct disorder may not do as well in treatment, as they sometimes struggle to maintain healthy relationships and to conform to rules. If your nonaddicted child is really misbehaving, being manipulative, or showing a disregard for others in any way, that might be reason to watch her carefully, as she might be at greater risk for developing addiction in the future.

ADHD and mental health issues, such as depression and anxiety, can be risk factors as well, though the link with addictions is not always robust.

Early drug use is another factor. The earlier that children start to use substances, the more likely they are to become addicted.

Use of drugs by immediate family members at home can be a risk factor, too, not just for addiction but for mental health problems such as anxiety. (This applies even to use of legal drugs, such as the nicotine in cigarettes.) A family history of addiction poses a higher risk that children will develop addiction.

Inconsistent messages about drug use in the home create risks as well. This is important. Parents are always asking me what they should tell their adolescent child who just started to use drugs. They want to know the magic words and whether they should be worried. Well, every family is different. Parents need to look at their own family history and relationships. They need to examine their child's previous history and their own parenting methods. When it comes to parenting methods, as I explain in part 1 of this book, the authoritative style works best. *Authoritative* means firm but emotionally responsive. This should not be confused with the *authoritarian* style, which is "do it my way or hit the highway."

In summary, most of us have vulnerabilities for some condition or problem in life. These might be risk factors for weight gain, diabetes, a gambling addiction, or something else. In the context of treating addiction, this means that a lot of factors need to be addressed simultaneously. These can include children's mental health issues and family problems—and even their emerging personalities. For instance, kids may have to learn how to

- take feedback from others and listen to others without dismissing their concerns
- be more flexible
- be more assertive
- control their anger
- demonstrate confidence while avoiding overconfidence

Such things are not necessarily captured in any diagnosis. These skills will not automatically be acquired through sobriety. Sobriety opens the door for progress, yet there is much more work to do.

Bottom line: *Recovery from addiction is a lifelong process. It begins with sobriety and continues with treatment that addresses a range of risk factors.*

Chapter 45

Hope for Change

When I was growing up, I admired those around me who were calm and laid back. Unfortunately, as much as I am chagrined to admit it, that wasn't me. Nobody likes to think of themselves as being high strung or lacking in patience, but that was me, as I look back on it. Of course, I didn't truly accept it then.

As I entered college, I decided that I wanted to be more laid back, too. So I grew my hair out and studied the neo-hippie styles, mannerisms, and musical tastes of a relaxed and carefree individual. It worked to some extent. People started to treat me differently. They wanted me to hang out in the back of the classroom. People who didn't know me would meet me for the first time and comment on my calm demeanor. I got invited to different kinds of activities. I actually wasn't that calm and wasn't nearly as laid back as I appeared. I looked the part, for sure, but in the end, I never really became the person I wanted to be. I still struggled with patience and calm.

Later in residency, the stresses of a high-pressure, sleep-deprived atmosphere pushed me to the brink. I had to find compassion at three in the morning in an emergency room while working with a belligerent and paranoid person coming down from cocaine, put aside my own fatigue and irritability to console a desperate family whose child overdosed at a party, and restrain bias in my clinical approach despite overwhelming evidence of an angry patient's criminal behaviors or checkered history. Under such conditions, it was easy to come face-to-face with my true strengths and deficits.

So it wasn't until my medical training that I accepted who I was as a person—gifts and limitations, all of it. And that acceptance of the painful inadequacies in my person finally led to real change.

Now when people meet me, I can be calm and patient, inside and out. I can be laid back without the hair or styling. I am still a work in progress, no doubt, and the less fruitful parts of my nature never completely go away. I realize now that those changes would never have occurred if I had not reconciled and embraced all parts of myself at one time or another.

To fix a problem adequately, it helps to first accept the degree of the problem itself. When it comes to personal growth, there are two basic ways to go about it. Some people choose to adopt high-minded principles and try to adhere to them religiously. Though the devotion is commendable, this is a tightrope of a journey that can lead to repeated disappointments. This approach can be as unrealistic as an out-of-shape person over-exerting himself at the gym after a long period of inactivity.

I would recommend the other approach. People who have a problem with anger must first embrace that part of themselves. I am not asking them to succumb to that trait. Instead, they should accept it and own it as a part of them. Then they are assured of the starting point in their journey, without delusions and without judgment. Improvements are now incremental but real. They learn to temper their maladaptive qualities as opposed to denying their existence.

When I work with young men who have abundant narcissism, for example (and many young men have some narcissism; this isn't entirely unhealthy in development), I advise them not to act like holy men when they discover humility. Instead, I ask them to accept that they have such a trait within and that it can be tempered and channeled for better effect. These young people may have to accept that they are naturally competitive, or that they need plenty of praise and accomplishments in their lives. The question, then, is how to fill those needs in a balanced and healthy manner that will support their recovery. That might mean volunteering or helping others out. It might mean being proactive about seeking fellowship in recovery. All of these endeavors provide sustenance for their needs in a positive way without creating strife or dissension. And that, in turn, provides the space for humility to blossom in the context of their own strengths and weaknesses.

As I close this book, I mention all of the above to provide hope for change in your child and your family. When reading a book like this, you might be disconcerted by some of the topics that you feel speak to your situation. *Oh no, that sounds like my child. That's exactly like my family. Uh-oh, that describes me.* Don't give up hope. Paradoxically, it is the acceptance of our need for growth and not a falsely devout pledge to an unattainable ideal that tills the fertile soil for therapeutic change. So take heart. Be brave. Own up to the things you do well and the things you struggle with. Start this parallel journey with your child with a sincere and open heart. Millions have, and millions will go on the same journey with you. No matter what your family has gone through, many others have taken a similar path and found a collective peace of mind.

Now is as good a time as any to start building the kind of culture you want for your family, one piece at a time. Remember to stay emotionally objective. Remember to be a leader first before being a friend. Remember to check your biases at the door. If you can do this, you will find that your love for your child, which once derailed your emotional balance, will now become the very fuel for your consistency. That discipline will lead to peace of mind. And in that frame of mind, you will find you are not alone.

Bottom line: *Acceptance is the first step of healthy change.*

About the Author

Joseph Lee, M.D., is the medical director for Hazelden's youth addiction services. Dr. Lee was born in Seoul, South Korea, but spent most of his youth in Norman, Oklahoma, where he went to college majoring in philosophy. After graduating from medical school, Dr. Lee completed his Adult Psychiatry residency at Duke University Hospital in Durham, North Carolina, and his fellowship in Child and Adolescent Psychiatry from Johns Hopkins Hospital in Baltimore, Maryland.

In addition to board certification from the American Board of Addiction Medicine, Dr. Lee is a leading national advocate for adolescent addiction and mental health issues. He serves as a spokesperson for the American Academy of Child and Adolescent Psychiatry on issues of addiction.

Dr. Lee currently resides in Minneapolis, Minnesota, with his wife, Jill, his son, Gabriel, and his annoying cockapoo, Jackson. You can follow him on Twitter@drjosephlee.

Hazelden, a national nonprofit organization founded in 1949, helps people reclaim their lives from the disease of addiction. Built on decades of knowledge and experience, Hazelden offers a comprehensive approach to addiction that addresses the full range of patient, family, and professional needs, including treatment and continuing care for youth and adults, research, higher learning, public education and advocacy, and publishing.

A life of recovery is lived "one day at a time." Hazelden publications, both educational and inspirational, support and strengthen lifelong recovery. In 1954, Hazelden published *Twenty-Four Hours a Day*, the first daily meditation book for recovering alcoholics, and Hazelden continues to publish works to inspire and guide individuals in treatment and recovery, and their loved ones. Professionals who work to prevent and treat addiction also turn to Hazelden for evidence-based curricula, informational materials, and videos for use in schools, treatment programs, and correctional programs.

Through published works, Hazelden extends the reach of hope, encouragement, help, and support to individuals, families, and communities affected by addiction and related issues.